1992

THE
ART NOUVEAU
STYLE

Les Maitres de l'Affiche PL 73
Imprimerie Chaix

THE ART NOUVEAU STYLE

Laurence Buffet-Challié

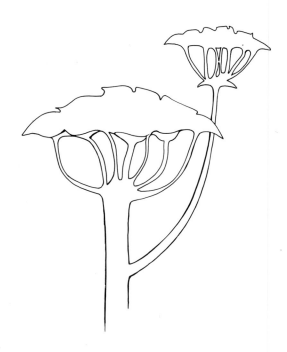

ACADEMY EDITIONS·LONDON

ACKNOWLEDGEMENTS

We wish to thank all those who have contributed to this book and who have provided valuable information; including Mr Cooper, Mrs C. Fenwick, M. Laforêt, Mme Legrand Kapferer, Mr and Mrs Robert Walker and Victor Arwas. Thanks also go to the following contributors of illustrative material: Allo Photo 178, 180-182; Archives d'Illustration 35, 270, 300; Chadefaux et Basnier 82, 83, 104, 112, 135, 137, 138, 140, 148, 162, 185, 272, 274, 390; Chadefaux 4, 6, 8-11, 13, 15, 37, 38, 40-44, 49, 50, 55, 57, 59, 65, 68-70, 77, 78, 105, 106, 110, 113, 114, 127, 166, 167, 169, 183, 190, 192-195, 233-235, 248, 252, 253, 257-266, 271, 273, 276-281, 283-285, 289, 291-293, 295, 298-309, 321, 325, 332, 334, 342, 345-348, 352-357, 369, 371-374, 376-378; Pierre Jahan 12, 39, 109, 117, 129, 170-172, 178, 222, 223, 286, 290, 341, 370, 376, 381, 384-389, 391-394; Boris Kebrer; Kollar 299; Mangin 16, 19-21, 26, 30, 31, 51, 54, 60-64, 66, 67, 123-127, 128, 164, 165, 186, 189, 286-288, 336, 349, 379, 380, 382; Musée des Arts Décoratifs, Paris 5, 7, 14, 25, 27, 29, 52, 53, 56, 69, 73, 74, 76, 79, 81, 99, 107, 111, 115, 173, 176, 177, 187, 298, 301, 302, 381; Nahmias 361, 362; Studio Contact 210, 217; Studio de Septenville 254, 324, 328-331; Laurent Sully-Jaulmes 88-97, 100, 101, 103, 108, 119-121, 184, 188, 211, 268, 375; Karin Szekssy 190; Top-Guillemot 161, 163, 243, 245, 282, 287, 320, 340, 358, 360, 363-365, 371; P. Hinous 132-136, 139, 226-228, 244, 367, Sotheby's Belgravia, London 131.

Front cover: EMILE GALLE *Aube et Crépuscule*, 1904, detail, carved opalescent glass, carved fruitwood and mother-of-pearl. See page 66. (Musée de l'Ecole de Nancy.)

Frontispiece: JULES CHERET Colour lithograph poster, *La Loïe Fuller aux Folies-Bergère*, 1893.

First published in Great Britain in 1982 by
Academy Editions 7/8 Holland Street London W8

First published in France by Baschet et Cie Paris
Translated from the French by Geoffrey Williams

Printed and bound in Hong Kong.

CONTENTS

INTRODUCTION

Those who were born towards the end of the nineteenth century witnessed an astonishing flowering of what came to be known in France as the Modern Style, but more generally as Art Nouveau.

The term 'flowering' aptly describes an art that was fundamentally inspired by nature. Hence the cultivation of a sense of intimacy in the second half of the nineteenth century by means of sombre wall-hangings, curtains overladen with trimmings, heavy upholstery and indoor gardens full of green plants, finally gave way to the need to observe the outside world. All decoration was henceforth inspired by the forms of branches, flowers and leaves. The straight line disappeared giving way to entanglements of convolvulus and ivy, to bouquets of iris and cow-parsley. Sculptors responded joyfully by intermingling the female body with forms of plant life and only tolerating a flat surface if it could be decorated with marquetry, depicting a landscape or flowers with the vividness of a painting. There was a sense of breaking free, of rejecting all styles derived from the past, of renouncing tired formulas that had been practised for too long. A new type of furniture appeared, like some mysterious plant springing up from the vegetation. Objects such as lamps and vases assumed the forms of the tulip, cyclamen and iris. Fabrics and wallpapers brought the colour and gaiety of flowers into the interior of the house, newly opened to the light of day. Such was the infatuation with nature that fashionable ladies were seen to appear sporting complete gardens on their heads, though they did not go so far as to abandon the restricting corset and other chastely garments which only the painters of the era had the daring to remove on canvas.

But flowerings are invariably short-lived and this one was particularly so. Very soon, even before the outbreak of the First World War, a reduced, simplified style began to appear, its triumph confirmed with the success of the International Exhibition of Decorative and Industrial Arts, held in Paris in 1925. The Modern Style, with its undulating lines, its profusion and imagery, suddenly became unbearable. Furniture and other objects, their value greatly reduced, were either relegated to attics or sold off cheaply.

But fashions tend to alternate and now, more than half a century later, Art Nouveau is being rescued from oblivion. At a time when the mass-production of goods from metals and synthetic materials is expanding, displacing further still the creative role of the craftsman, it is not surprising that a style rooted in fantasy and spontaneity should be asserting itself anew. And so the attics have yielded up their testimony of lost time to a second life: bric-à-brac drawn from the dust is transformed into treasure to be fought over by the collectors. Even the Métro gratings that have disappeared one by one from the streets of Paris are now being haggled over not only in France but abroad as well. Entire houses and apartments are furnished in the Art Nouveau style by antique dealers specialising in the 1900 period. The purpose of this book is thus to introduce the enthusiast to a closer acquaintance with the artists whose names have suddenly emerged from the past and to familiarise him with the very varied techniques of an art which, having made such a strong appeal to the imagination, scarcely deserved to be so rapidly extinguished.

2 Salon in *La Garenne,* the home of Emile Gallé, c.1900. (Private Collection)

3 EUGENE GRASSET   Illustration from *La Plante et ses applications ornementales*, 1897.

THE ORIGINS
OF ART NOUVEAU

Of the Art Nouveau period Le Corbusier wrote: 'The spirit was on fire'. A blaze of invention, fantasy and audacity in the realm of decorative art spread to engulf all the Western nations. Art Nouveau in England, Modern Style in France, Jugendstil in Germany, Secessionstil in Austria — the appellations were as numerous as the derisory nicknames invented by its critics: Noodle Style, Métro Style, Tapeworm Style, Lily Style (Lilienstil). These movements were all based on what was fundamentally a common inspiration, though there were some striking differences between individual artists and countries. Art Nouveau was at once homespun and exotic, literary and plastic, mystical and erotic, futurist and traditional, functional and fantastic. It was a perfect illustration of the Hegelian system of contraries, extolled by Oscar Wilde, whereby an artistic truth is only valid if its opposite is equally true.

It was in England, the most industrially advanced country, that the first signs of a reaction appeared. John Ruskin (1819-1900) conceived of the machine as a source of nothing but ugliness and despair. Only the hand of man could imbue matter with beauty and life. It was necessary, without aspiring to actually copy him, to rediscover the mentality of the mediaeval craftsman, inspired by faith and the love of nature. Every distinction between the major and minor arts was to be abolished. Ruskin appointed himself leader of the Pre-Raphaelite painters who were driven by the same ideal: Beauty within the grasp of all. Ruskin's theories were put into practice by two members of this group, Edward Burne-Jones (1833-1898) and above all, William Morris (1834-1896), who abandoned painting to devote himself to the embellishment of the home. An early example of a commercial organisation concerned with both production and distribution was that of Morris-Marshall-Faulkner, founded in 1861, which flooded England and subsequently Europe with its products: furniture, fabrics, wallpaper, ceramics and stained glass, all conceived with a new sense of decorative unity. The formula was taken up with equal success by Arthur Lazenby Liberty. The work of the following generation, Arthur Heygate Mackmurdo (1851-1942), Charles Annesley Voysey (1857-1941) and above all Charles Rennie Mackintosh (1868-1928), who founded the Glasgow group, moved away from the lyricism of the Pre-Raphaelites. Their simplified, almost austere sense of structure prefigured a tendency that was to blossom with the Bauhaus.

In Barcelona, Antonio Gaudi (1852-1926) surrendered to a delirious obsession with ornamentation. In Belgium, three architects and decorators, Paul Hankar (1859-1901), Victor Horta (1861-1947) and Henry van de Velde (1863-1957), who were primarily concerned with the curve, created the 'whiplash line'. Such writers as Lemonnier, Maeterlinck and Verhaeren made Brussels the capital city of Symbolism, the literary movement which influenced the fin-de-siècle aesthetic more than any other. It was a confusing movement, in which ideas dissolved into dreams, music and poetry into melodious çadences, plastic creation into an undulating line. Aubrey Beardsley in England, Fernand Khnopff in Belgium, Gustav Klimt in Austria and Gustave Moreau in Paris all laid particular stress on this ambiguity. In France Symbolism and Decadence were both complementary and opposed; one 'dedicated to the people', the other 'aristocratic'. The meanderings of Jean Lorrain, des Esseintes, Robert de Montesquiou and the posters of Mucha and Chéret, captured the neurotic chimeras of the Belle Epoque. The preoccupation with pale, sinuous women with flowing, disordered hair and with flowers and snakes, reached obsessive proportions. Disturbing creatures were abroad, painted in 'lilac turned to white' (J.K. Huysmans, 1883) and draped in the 'green mourning of love' (Maeterlinck).

The fascination with Gothic art and the mediaeval craftsman was largely due to the influence of Eugène Viollet-le-Duc (1814-1879). Condemned as an imitator, he was in reality an innovator, an advocate of dynamic, organic structures that were the opposite of the static architecture of classicism and of the use of iron as an indispensable material for modern building. He influenced Antonio Gaudi, Hector Guimard and, indirectly, the Ecole de Nancy.

A pupil of Viollet-le-Duc, the architect and designer of ornamental forms, Eugène Grasset (1841-1917) produced a curious synthesis of mediaevalism, naturalism and Japanese art. His work on *La Plante et ses applications ornementales* is a veritable bible of decoration that exalts the cult of Flora. The engraver, Félix Bracquemond (1883-1914) introduced him to Japanese prints which had just begun to appear in Europe. Grasset's enthusiasm infected his friends, painters and writers alike, who included Manet, Degas, Baudelaire and, above all, the Goncourts, who were ardent disciples of this art.

The influence of the Far East, Japan and China affected not only painters but decorators, cabinet-makers, ceramists and glassmakers. The role played by the celebrated dealer and collector, Samuel Bing, in the dissemination of this trend, when he opened his gallery, L'Art Nouveau, in Paris will be discussed later. But it was at Nancy, under the aegis of Emile Gallé, that the Japanese influence, combined with floralism and a hint of remembered Rococo, was transformed into a distinctive, personal style that was of prime importance in the unfolding of the Art Nouveau style.

FURNITURE

L'ECOLE DE NANCY

EMILE GALLE

From the middle of the nineteenth century, the furniture trade in France had become increasingly moribund, relying on a parody of traditional styles and an eclectic historicism which encompassed a medley of Classical, Gothic, Renaissance, Baroque and Rococo themes. In addition, the machine tool had caused the disappearance of the specialised craftsman who might have created new models. A reaction naturally set in, the impetus coming not from the cabinet-makers but from architects, painters and sculptors, based surprisingly in the provincial town of Nancy.

In 1884, Emile Gallé (1846-1904), already the head of an established ceramics and glassmaking concern, inaugurated a new branch of his activities: cabinet-making. This vocation sprang from a visit to a dealer in exotic woods where, excited by the range of colours and textures, the young Gallé decided to experiment with woodwork. The guiding principles behind this new activity were simple: a piece of furniture had to be logically constructed and designed to concord with its function. 'In so far as concerns the shaping of the frame,' wrote Gallé, 'we have but a simple choice between traditional contours and those taken from flora and fauna.' Nature was inspirational, hence the appearance of 'dragonfly', 'cow-parsley' and 'vine-stock' table legs, 'waterlily' pedestals and 'banana-tree' plant stands. When produced with the aid of mechanical equipment, these plant forms had to be rendered in a simplified form; a foot displaying the outline of a thistle, a colonette in the form of a poppy-pod, intertwined convolvulus or forms derived from the orchid or hogweed.

Gallé normally worked in soft woods, preferably of local or European origin, which were well suited for carving. This enabled him, on some of his more luxurious models, to resolve the delicate problem of the joints by means of natural carved attachments, often of maple wood.

This passion for naturalism culminated in the ornamentation of flat surfaces, on which Gallé lavished every attention. In most instances he personally designed the motifs that were to be reproduced in marquetry, composed of incrustations of precious woods in refined tones. The entire flora of Lorraine was brought to life in these dazzling displays of decorative invention.

Very often the decoration and the structure were complementary so that the stems of the plant reproduced in marquetry also formed the supporting structure of the work, transforming it into a wild vegetation rising up from the floor. But Gallé was not merely a poetic soul inspired by nature for he possessed the sense of precision of the botanist and the entomologist and the scientific knowledge associated with these two disciplines. Describing a table designed for a country house 'with polychrome decor of polished wood incrusted with ash and floral ornamentation drawn from the plant life of Alsace-Lorraine', he enumerates not only the different plants; muscari comosum, anemone nemorosa, orchis bifolia, narcissus poeticus, but the exact location in which each had been found. Japanese art constituted another source of inspiration for Gallé had first been attracted to the Far East in London at the 1871 Exhibition. Chrysanthemums, clusters of dragonflies, bamboo, irises and waterlilies bear witness to his knowledge of oriental themes and his ability to translate them with stirring sensitivity. To these influences can be added a poetic symbolism that was close to Gallé's heart. Quotations from Hugo, Verlaine, Baudelaire, Maeterlinck, Mallarmé, Rodenbach and Sully-Prud'homme were inscribed in marquetry alongside the decorations. He wanted his furniture to be not only 'alive', or inspired by life, but also to 'speak', to make intimations of 'certain visions of transcendental shapes and forms which dwell in the realms of desire and imagination' — a literary approach which he had already applied to his glass vases.

This prolific but graceful ornamentation successfully expresses the aesthetic, social and philosophical aspirations of its creator. Unfortunately it sometimes masks the structure of the work, contrary to the rules of furniture making and does not always comply with Gallé's professed concern for logic and practicality. A taste for naturalism and symbolism triumphed over the rational and the principles of balance and form were often neglected. The first pieces of furniture produced by Gallé, displayed in Paris at the International Exhibition of 1889, enjoyed, nonetheless, a considerable success. The originality of their conception provided a striking contrast with conventional productions and marked a revival of the spirit of craftsmanship. The smaller tables, for instance, attracted a large number of orders which the workshops of Nancy had difficulty in meeting. A large table that dates from this period and bears some very vivid marquetry based on a design by Victor Prouvé, a friend and associate of Gallé, can be found in the Musée de l'Ecole de Nancy. A console, *Les Parfums d'Autrefois* (1894) reinterprets the grace and excellence of an eighteenth-century creation in a spirit typical of the Art Nouveau of Nancy. On the front panel the vein of the wood simulates a moving sky and poetic inscriptions are intertwined with wild flowers and inlaid with the finesse of a watercolourist. Curved lines are elaborated with elegantly carved plant forms and a melting iridescent patina envelops the whole. If Gallé was rejecting imitation he nevertheless recognised the refinement of a tradition. Towards the end of his life, Gallé broke away from the mannerism of his early works and asserted a preference for less agitated forms. At the same time his inclination towards symbolism grew more pronounced; the bed *Aube et Crepuscule*, executed for a friend, the magistrate Henri Hirsch, clearly illustrating this

development. Although suffering from leukaemia, Gallé still insisted in directing the proceedings from his armchair. The sumptuous butterflies inlaid on the bedheads evoke more than just the ephemeral quality of day or the mysteries of night. Their huge wings dusted with mother-of-pearl, surrounding an opalescent glass egg testify to the perpetual rhythm of life in this, possibly the most fantastic of all Art Nouveau creations.

Apart from the essential items, Gallé created innumerable small pieces of furniture; occasional tables, étagères, screens, nests of tables, bedside tables, music cabinets, embroidery frames and plant stands, all of which gave free reign to his imaginative zest. The majority of these pieces, however, form part of his industrial production and are not always of good quality. For this reason he did not succeed in producing the social art to which he aspired. But the greater part of his personal production was incontestably successful, since it was clearly the expression of an artistic spirit of sincerity, idealism and generosity.

4 EMILE GALLE Rectangular table with marquetry work. (Private Collection)

5

6

7

5 EMILE GALLE Moulded and carved beechwood canapé.
(Musée des Arts Décoratifs, Paris)

6 EMILE GALLE Chair with cow-parsley motif. (Collection
Alain Lesieutre, Paris)

7 EMILE GALLE Chair and stool with cow-parsley motif.
(Musée des Arts Décoratifs, Paris)

8-11 EMILE GALLE Tables with details of the marquetry
work clearly showing Gallé's signature. (Private Collection)

8

9

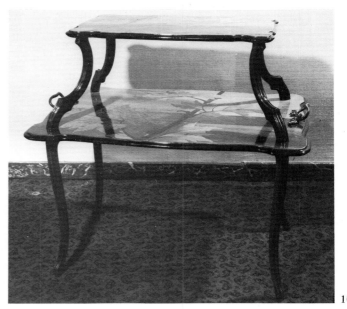

10

11

12

13

14

12 EMILE GALLE   Nest of tables and firescreen. (Musée de l'Ecole de Nancy)

13 EMILE GALLE   A characteristic example of a piece of furniture where the legs and crossbar resemble parts of a tree – in this case, the cherry. (Collection Alain Lesieutre, Paris)

14 EMILE GALLE   Walnut plant stand with marquetry surfaces. (Musée des Arts Décoratifs, Paris)

15 EMILLE GALLE   Occasional table decorated with the cow-parsley motif on which rest a lamp and a vase also by Gallé. (Collection Jean-Claude Brugnot)

16 EMILE GALLE   Tea table with marquetry designs. (Collection Félix Marcilhac, Paris)

17 EMILE GALLE   Characteristic table 'aux libellules'. (Musée de l'Ecole de Nancy)

18 EMILE GALLE   Pedestal table inspired by natural forms. (Musée de l'Ecole de Nancy)

15

16

17

18

19

20

21

19-21 EMILE GALLE Examples of marquetry work and detailed wood carving. (Musée de l'Ecole de Nancy)

22 EMILE GALLE Display cabinet with carved cow-parsley motif and inlaid back panel. (Private Collection, New York)

23 EMILE GALLE Small commode with two drawers. (Private Collection)

24 EMILE GALLE Landscapes are often to be found on Gallé's work but few as beautiful as the winter scene on this chest. (Collection Félix Marcilhac, Paris)

22

23

24

26

25

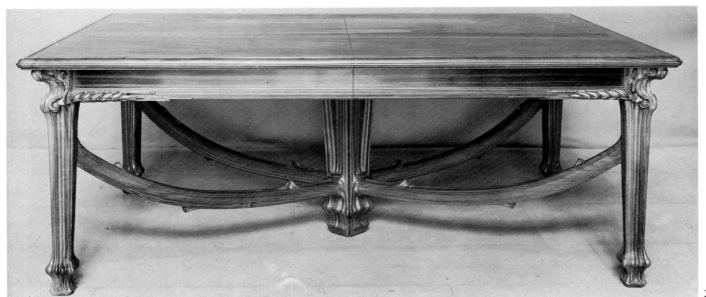

27

28

25 EMILE GALLE Walnut sideboard with carved ears of corn and landscapes inlaid in wood. (Musée de l'Ecole de Nancy)

26 EMILE GALLE Signature inlaid in wood.

27 EMILE GALLE Walnut dining table with polychrome wood inlay and carved, gilt-bronze ornamentation. (Musée des Arts Décoratifs, Paris)

28 EMILE GALLE Sideboard on the theme of autumn, 1903. (Private Collection, New York)

29

30

31

32

29 EMILE GALLE Walnut screen framing embroidered Chinese silk. (Musée des Arts Décoratifs, Paris)

30 EMILE GALLE Etagère inspired by many of the forms of nature in a Chinese style. (Musée de l'Ecole de Nancy)

31 EMILE GALLE Shelves with cow-parsley motif, central cupboard and inlaid door. (Musée de l'Ecole de Nancy)

32 EMILE GALLE Etagère based on the cow-parsley motif, 1900.

33 Bed and loom by Emile André and chair by Louis Majorelle. (Musée de l'Ecole de Nancy)

33

LOUIS MAJORELLE

The group of artists which formed around Emile Gallé was to make an important contribution to the renown of the Ecole de Nancy (formally constituted in 1901). Of this group it was Louis Majorelle (1859-1926) who was to become one of its leading figures. After studying painting in Paris as a pupil of Millet, Majorelle returned to Nancy to manage the family furnishing business following the premature death of his father. There he was introduced to cabinet-making by his own craftsmen, quickly mastering all of the technical difficulties and by 1897 had rallied to the cause of Art Nouveau.

Majorelle was certainly influenced by Gallé, yet by comparison his manner speaks more of the technician than the poet. 'Nature', he wrote, 'is a wonderful collaborator, an inexhaustible source of decorative motifs. But it must not be allowed to dictate the form of a piece of furniture ... A sumptuous effect should not be sought by means of unbridled profusion but by elegance of line and a sense of proportion.

The modern cabinet-maker cannot ignore the principles of architectural construction discovered by his predecessors.' This respect for the past is evident in certain chairs, particularly the gilded wooden armchairs decorated with pinecones in the Musée de Nancy. But this sensitive adaptation of the Louis XV style, free of any suggestion of pastiche, is only one aspect of his work, and in no way detracts from the title of 'The Cressent of Art Nouveau' bestowed on him by M. Rheims in *L'Art 1900*. (Charles Cressent, one of the leading cabinet-makers of the eighteenth century, embellished his work with bronze ornamentation).

Majorelle became known to a wider public at the 1900 Exhibition where, as a disciple of the Ecole de Nancy, he displayed a writing-desk decorated with bronze waterlilies. His best furniture was produced between 1902 and 1906 and is distinguished by its impeccable execution and a supple, restrained sense of design that harmonises perfectly with its function. It is curved in accordance with the demands of comfort and the legs, often doubled at the foot and stressed by means of bronze ornamentation, strengthen the structure without compromising the delicacy of line. Two very typical Art Nouveau flowers, the waterlily and the orchid, are invariably incorporated into the bronze embellishments, as perfectly executed as those of the great bronzesmiths of the eighteenth century. Majorelle was also very interested in the possibilities of iron and established his own workshop where he created not only appendages for his furniture but complete banisters such as those for the great stairway of the Galeries Lafayette in Paris.

Most of his furniture was built in such hard woods as mahogany or Brazilian rosewood which do not lend themselves easily to sculpture. Their rich brown tones do, however, serve to display the frequent appendages of gilt-bronze to full advantage. Though Majorelle rarely produced sculpture it cannot be said that he neglected marquetry, with which he gave full reign to his penchant for a naturalism that was free from the symbolist associations characteristic of Emile Gallé's approach. Many of these small pieces of furniture with marquetry work were conceived as sets but nowadays, it is his furniture decorated with his distinctive waterlily or orchid bronzes that are so highly prized among contemporary collectors.

Majorelle continued to explore new creative ideas until 1914 whilst his workshop was simultaneously operating along more industrial lines to meet the demands of a less wealthy clientele. A number of retail workshops were even opened in Paris to sell a simplified, standardised type of furniture of no more than marginal interest, though it nonetheless conformed to the aesthetic principles propounded by its creator.

34 LOUIS MAJORELLE Mahogany table with raised areas of copper gilt. (Musée des Arts Décoratifs, Paris)

34

35

36

35 LOUIS MAJORELLE Desk and chairs executed for the Paris 1925 Exhibition showing the development towards a simpler, less ornamental style.

36 LOUIS MAJORELLE Carved and inlaid cabinet inspired by natural forms. (Collection Félix Marcilhac, Paris)

37 LOUIS MAJORELLE Carved wooden screen painted by Girardet. (Private Collection)

38 LOUIS MAJORELLE Small sideboard 'aux pissenlits' and two vases by Bigot and Bourdelle. The picture on the wall entitled *La Druidesse* is by Gabriel Ferrier. (Private Collection)

39 LOUIS MAJORELLE Bedroom furniture.

37

38

39

40

41

42

40-41 LOUIS MAJORELLE Cabinet with inlaid flower design and detail of its carved convolvulus.

42 LOUIS MAJORELLE Small triangular table with a vase by Lentz and box by Chéret. (Private Collection)

44

3

43 LOUIS MAJORELLE Chair with copper highlights on the base of the feet.

44 LOUIS MAJORELLE Morning-room containing chairs and a pedestal table.
(Collection Manoukian, Paris)

45

45 LOUIS MAJORELLE   Chair.

46 LOUIS MAJORELLE   Dining-room furnished entirely in mahogany and macassar ebony.

47 LOUIS MAJORELLE   Detail of the doors of the sideboard with large gilt-bronze ornamentation.

48 LOUIS MAJORELLE   Pewter clock face with copper numbers. (Collection M. and Mme B.)

46

47

48

49

50

VICTOR PROUVE

Besides being a painter, engraver and sculptor, Victor Prouvé (1858-1943) was also one of the most eminent personalities of the Ecole de Nancy. He designed vase decorations and projects for marquetry work for Gallé, Majorelle and Vallin. Four pieces of furniture that he had helped to produce appeared in the 1889 Exhibition, including a cabinet entitled *Le Chêne lorrain, oeuvre française*, and a large table decorated with marquetry based on a theme of Tacitus – *Le Rhin sépare des Gaules toute la Germanie*. Such nationalistic themes reflected the strongly patriotic feelings of these young artists. Gallé

was very pleased and congratulated Prouvé. 'Your table is a masterpiece, a page of history. I have made every effort to provide a modest little flute accompaniment worthy of your bassoon.' Three baby grand pianos designed by Majorelle, with marquetry conceived by Prouvé, are also worthy of note. When Gallé died in 1904, Prouvé was made president of the Ecole de Nancy but not, as has often been alleged, artistic director of Gallé's organisation, in which he never occupied any official post.

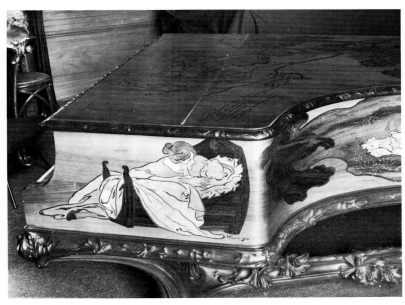

49 LOUIS MAJORELLE   Display cabinet with bronze ornamentation containing a collection of Art Nouveau vases and bronzes. (Collection Alain Lesieutre, Paris)

50 LOUIS MAJORELLE   Small display cabinet, the upper portion of which forms a niche. (Collection Manoukian, Paris)

51 LOUIS MAJORELLE   Detail of a piano with marquetry work by Gallé. (Musée de l'Ecole de Nancy)

52-53 LOUIS MAJORELLE   Piano with detail of the marquetry work by Gallé based on designs by Victor Prouvé. (Musée des Arts Décoratifs, Paris)

54

55

56

57

58

59

54 LOUIS MAJORELLE Salon with gilt-wood chairs in the Musée de l'Ecole de Nancy.

55 LOUIS MAJORELLE Small travailleuse. (Collection Manoukian, Paris)

56 LOUIS MAJORELLE Mahogany and leather chair. (Musée des Arts Décoratifs, Paris)

57 LOUIS MAJORELLE Cabinet with marquetry landscape. (Collection Maria de Beyrie)

58 LOUIS MAJORELLE Bedside cabinet with bronze ornamentation in the form of leaves and waterlily stems. (Collection Maria de Beyrie)

59 LOUIS MAJORELLE Two-tiered table inlaid with flower designs and with a single bronze motif. (Collection Alain Lesieutre, Paris)

EUGENE VALLIN

Eugène Vallin (1856-1925) was a close friend of Louis Majorelle and Victor Prouvé and well schooled in a variety of technical matters. He was a carpenter, specialist in church furniture and restorer of buildings who had a profound admiration for Viollet-le-Duc and in particular for his *Dictionnaire d'Architecture*. He was taken on by Gallé to create modern furniture as a member of the Ecole de Nancy. Vallin's creations are small in number but possess a commanding sense of the bulk and powerfulness of line that is suggestive, like Gothic architecture, of burgeoning plant life. They look as if they have been cut straight from the trunk and their beauty lies in the generous rhythms of the wood, the warmth of tone and the care with which they are fashioned. The solidity of the supports, and the majesty of the proportions set them apart from Gallé's poetic symbolism and 'diaphanous' art.

The Musée de Nancy contains a dining-room by Vallin, one of the most typical of Art Nouveau ensembles, preserved in accordance with its original conception. Indissociable from nineteenth-century society, the dining-room incarnates the bourgeois myth of easeful living. Vallin's furniture satisfied the tastes of a clientele who liked to entertain and make an opulent display of its wealth. 'It combines', noted Mlle Thérèse Charpentier, 'the rationalism of Viollet-le-Duc with the solid traditions of craftmanship embodied in the great wooden chests of Lorraine, while the plant-like curves rendered in exotic woods, such as citron, are reminiscent of the eighteenth century'. The leather murals, and the ceiling and carvings by Victor Prouvé complement the arrangement with an added sense of refinement.

60

61

62

63

60-61 EUGENE VALLIN Original design and finished sideboard for a dining-room. (Musée de l'Ecole de Nancy)

62 EUGENE VALLIN An example of the use of curved lines in Vallin's furniture.

63 EUGENE VALLIN Fireplace which blends with the woodwork from the dining-room on the opposite page.

64 EUGENE VALLIN Design for windows and display cabinets.

64

JACQUES GRUBER

Jacques Grüber (1870-n.d.) holder of a bursary from the town of Nancy, was a pupil of Gustave Moreau in Paris. Appointed professor of decorative arts at the Ecole des Beaux-Arts in Nancy, Grüber quickly adopted Gallé's ideas. He was active in several domains: mural painting, furniture, glass-work, fabrics, embroidery and finally, stained glass. Amongst the furniture and ensembles that he designed there figures, in the Musée de Nancy, a dining-room executed for Professor Etienne of the Faculty of Medicine at Nancy. These large pieces of furniture, their ascendant rhythms rendered by a rather insubstantial curved linearity, do not possess the baroque vitality of Vallin's creations, though they come close to it. Little glass windows of glowing red lend warmth to these sober architectural forms of mediaeval inspiration. The sense of bulk characteristic of Vallin is sometimes also apparent with Grüber, as in the case of an imposing financier's desk decorated with bronze ferns. The dominating appearance of the desk, no doubt insisted upon by the customer, is combined with the fragility of the plant motif — implying that the social and naturalistic aims of the craftsmen were not always in accord with the opulent aspirations of a bourgeois rationalist clientele.

A number of other artists figure amongst those who were creating furniture of the Ecole de Nancy: the architect Emile André, Gauthier and Pointsignon, Ferez, Neiss and Schwartz, all of whom were anxious to put into practice the principle of the unity of art, and to contribute to an artistic revival by means of naturalism and the practice of local traditions.

65

65 JACQUES GRUBER and LOUIS MAJORELLE Firescreen. (Collection Manoukian, Paris)

66 JACQUES GRUBER Room setting emphasising the use of curved lines taken from nature. The armchairs are by Majorelle. (Musée de l'Ecole de Nancy)

66

67 JACQUES GRUBER Large sideboard. (Musée de l'Ecole de Nancy)

BING AND ART NOUVEAU

Paris followed Nancy's lead in the great modern art movement that developed in France and several other European countries towards the end of the nineteenth century. Official efforts to stimulate this renewal (such as the creation in 1862 of the Union des Beaux-Arts appliqués à l'Industrie and the foundation in 1878 of the Musée des Arts Décoratifs, established to promote competitions) were all well co-ordinated but did not succeed in their aim of motivating the artists and craftsmen.

The stimulus came, as at Nancy, from the spirit of enterprise of one man, Samuel Bing (1838-1905). Maecenas, dealer, orientalist and editor of a remarkable revue, *Le Japon artistique*, Bing was converted to the new trends after a trip to the United States. In 1895 he decided to convert his antique shop in the rue de Provence into the Galerie de L'Art Nouveau. A priori, his aim does not appear to be revolutionary: 'To energetically combat the crazy pretension of breaking with the past. All the work of our forefathers stands as an example before our eyes, not, to be sure, to be taken as a model for base and servile imitations, but rather as the source of an inspiration that is derived from the spirit of its conception. . . We must reimmerse ourselves in the ancient French traditions and endeavour to pick up the threads of that tradition, its grace, elegance, purity and sound logic and enrich our heritage with a lively spirit of modernity.' This rather nationalistic profession of faith did not prevent Bing from displaying and selling the creations of foreign artists, notably the glasswork of the American, Louis Comfort Tiffany. The international dimension differentiates Paris as a centre of Art Nouveau from Nancy which was strictly regional.

Bing not only aspired to bring together all the elements that form a modern interior such as painting, furniture, hangings, objets d'art and d'usage. He also opened his own workshops where the best craftsmen of the age vied for honours: Georges de Feure, Eugène Gaillard, Edward Colonna — protean artists who exercised their talents in several fields. Like Gallé, Bing did not separate the applied arts of painting, sculpture and architecture.

The Bing Pavilion at the 1900 Exhibition
At the 1900 Exhibition, on the Esplanade des Invalides and surrounded by some rather bizarre constructions, Bing presented a pavilion devoted to Art Nouveau. The principal members of his team, de Feure, Gaillard and Colonna, participated in its realisation. It consisted of a six-room house with an interior decoration arrangement that brought together the best work of these young artists. In the drawing-room Colonna decorated the wall panels of lemonwood with green plush. This classical sobriety was echoed by the restrained, unelaborated style of the furniture which was also in lemonwood. The dining-room and bedroom, conceived by Gaillard in pearwood and ash combined architectural rigour with the soft rhythms of curves. De Feure's boudoir, a 'retreat decked with gold, silk and flowers' was a triumphant success, as was his 'cabinet de toilette' hung with panels of grey-blue brocaded silk decorated with grey-mauve and grey-green motifs that evoked 'flower-filled fields in the moonlight'. The success, with both the public and the critics, was considerable.

The Maison Moderne
Founded in 1897 by a German art critic, Julius Meier-Graefe, the Maison Moderne emulated Bing's Art Nouveau, but in a standardised, industrialised form. Abel Landry, architect and decorator, assumed responsibility for its direction but his furniture only constituted a banal reworking of the creations of the masters of Nancy and Paris. The aim in every instance was to produce 'only that which has been ennobled by Art with the prestige of Beauty'. The Maison Moderne also dealt in objets d'art, small sculptures, jewellery and ceramics (notably the Danish products of Bing and Gröndahl). Some excellent artists, including Tony Selmersheim, Maurice Dufrêne, Paul Follot, Félix Aubert, Clément Mère and Georges Lemmen, designed items for this business.

EUGENE GAILLARD

Eugène Gaillard (1862-1933) was a creator of 'engineer's furniture' who was more interested in solid, logical structures than decoration, to the exclusion of any explicitly figurative representations of plants or flowers. The leaves and stems of water-plants inspired him with their supple forms: straight lines and curves combined to form long ribbons of real plastic beauty. These inventions were never gratuitous since they served to render the seated position as comfortable as possible; thus the back of the chair is never stiff and comfortably supports the back. It is often slightly padded with the lower part left open, while the seat is coil-spung and covered in leather. The fluid and unbroken lines do not compromise the impression of solidity which Gaillard achieved mostly through the use of such hard woods as mahogany, Brazilian rosewood and walnut, but also pear and ash. He expounded his notions of form in a work entitled *A Propos du mobilier.*

68

69

68 EUGENE GAILLARD   Table, chair and plant stand with glazed stoneware plate by Clément Massier on the wall, sculpture by Bernhart Hoetger and porcelain vase by Auguste Delaherche. (Private Collection)

69 EUGENE GAILLARD   Mahogany and leather chair.

71

70

72

70 EUGENE GAILLARD Cane fireside chair (Collection Manoukian, Paris)

71 EUGENE GAILLARD Desk chair. (Collection Félix Marcilhac, Paris)

72 EUGENE GAILLARD Two-tiered tea table. (Collection Félix Marcilhac, Paris)

73 EUGENE GAILLARD Mahogany and embossed leather chair.

74 EUGENE GAILLARD Brazilian rosewood chair upholstered in 'pluie d'or' silk. (Musée des Arts Décoratifs, Paris)

75 EUGENE GAILLARD Tea table with removable trays.

76 EUGENE GAILLARD Large display cabinet. (Musée des Arts Décoratifs, Paris)

FURNITURE

73

74

75

76

78

77 EUGENE GAILLARD Pearwood desk and chair made c.1905 with a Daum lamp.

78 EUGENE GAILLARD Display cabinet on which rest two vases by Daum, an iridescent vase by Loetz and a candlestick by de Feure. (Private Collection)

79 EUGENE GAILLARD Brazilian rosewood canapé. (Musée des Arts Décoratifs, Paris)

79

GEORGES DE FEURE

Georges de Feure (1868-1928) was one of the more versatile and extravagant figures of Art Nouveau. A painter and poet, his work reflects the satanic spirit of Aubrey Beardsley, Baudelaire or Edgar Poe, 'perfumed with opium and morbid blooms'. The majority of his creations, whether in porcelain, glass, silver, stained glass, fabrics, wallpaper or light fittings, betray the same disturbing aesthetic. His furniture and interior decorations possess an elegance reminiscent of the late decorative style of the Trianon and thus follow the views of Bing by fusing tradition and modernity. A refined colourist, De Feure liked to gild and lacquer his woods in tones of dull green, mauve and light blue. His chairs reflect the decorative arabesques of insects and plants: the head of a canapé is transformed into the spreading wings of a butterfly; armrests follow the supple forms of plants and dainty feet are connected to the seat by means of luxurious sculpted creepers. But stylisation nevertheless triumphs over naturalism. De Feure was above all an aesthete and surrounded himself with greyhounds which he loved to depict in his compositions along with the languid, undulating forms of women draped in prurient attire.

80 GEORGES DE FEURE Chair. (Collection Knut Günther)

81 GEORGES DE FEURE Carved and gilt-wood screen with embroidery by Anaïs Favre. (Musée des Arts Décoratifs, Paris)

80

81

EDWARD COLONNA

Edward Colonna (1862-1948) born near Cologne, emigrated in 1882 to the United States where he worked with a group of decorators under the direction of Tiffany. From 1898 to 1903 Colonna, having returned to Paris, designed furniture, interiors, porcelain and fabrics for Bing. Although his works were small in number he emerges today as an accomplished practitioner of Art Nouveau. As a creator of interiors he presented in the Pavillon Bing de l'Art Nouveau at the 1900 Exhibition drawing-room furniture in lemonwood of almost classical appearance.

Léon Jallot, the creator of ornamentations, also collaborated with Bing. He designed furniture with simple linear forms, free from the associations of historicism or symbolism and even approached abstraction in the use of naturalistic motifs.

82 EDWARD COLONNA Lemonwood display cabinet, once part of the Salon of Suzanne Bing. (Hamburg Museum)

83 EDWARD COLONNA Chair from the same suite of furniture.

84 EDWARD COLONNA Table. (Collection Félix Marcilhac, Paris)

82

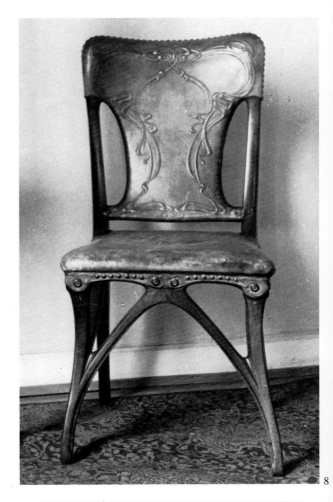

8

8

ARCHITECTS AND THEIR FURNITURE

L'Art dans tout

Beauty combined with Utility: this concept was fundamental to Art Nouveau and it induced a number of artists to join together to promote their cause. Alexandre Charpentier, sculptor and ornamental designer, Jean Dampt, sculptor, Félix Aubert, sculptor and designer, Tony Selmersheim, architect and Etienne Moreau-Nelaton, ceramist, founded in 1895 the Group of Five, which, the following year, with the arrival of the architect Charles Plumet, became the Group of Six. In 1897, the sculptor, Henri Nocq and the architect, Henri Sauvage, united to form the group which was to be known as L'Art dans tout.

Alexandre Charpentier (1856-1909) filled with enthusiasm for Art Nouveau, exercised his considerable sculptural talent in the field of the applied arts. The restraint of his early works gave way towards 1890, to a more exuberant rendering of line and sculpted panels with nude figures. But he always stopped short of over-elaboration, even when adding bronze plaques to his furniture – (a decorative process which he applied with equal success to his bookbindings).

The creations of Jean-Auguste Dampt (1853-1946) are marked by a symbolism that draws on the Baroque. His sculpture is closely integrated into the furniture – a tendency that was to be affirmed by Rupert Carabin. The architect, Charles Plumet (1861-1928) erected a number of buildings, including luxurious town houses. Hostile towards symbolism and in favour of a 'functionalist' approach, he created multi-purpose furniture, such as his canapé – display cabinet – bookcase. Plumet united the qualities of force, gracefulness and dynamism following the example of the Belgian 'whip-lash' style.

Pierre and Tony Selmersheim also created furniture designed for multiple use, combining painstaking construction and a delicate architectural sense with a hint of nostalgia.

Georges Hoentschel (1855-1915), architect and ceramist, is best known for his Salle du Bois from the Pavillon de l'Union Centrale des Arts Décoratifs at the 1900 Exhibition. He produced all of the panelling and some furniture of a markedly naturalistic style. His conception of decoration excluded any tendency towards stylisation for he was the ultimate defender of the imitation, pure and simple, of nature.

HECTOR GUIMARD

The celebrated architect Hector Guimard (1867-1942) was the most fervent adept of the unity of art. Not a single detail nor a line of his architecture, interior decoration or furniture was conceived other than as an intrinsic part of the whole. Logic, harmony and sensibility are the governing principles of all his work. His first successfully completed project, the Castel Béranger (1897-1898), was an affirmation of his desire for unity and the few pieces of furniture that he produced conformed also to this same ideal. No concessions were made to fashionable naturalism or to symbolism, no matter what the circumstances might dictate.

The art of Hector Guimard lies essentially in its graphic quality, in linear developments that spring from the ground, winding boldly upwards into space. By means of this line the organic impulse is transformed into pure abstraction. References to nature in the form of fruits, flowers and leaves are always discreet and never constitute a theme; stems and sea-plants serve only as inspiration for the sinuous motions of his creations. Curves and straight lines intertwine and stretch without disturbing their equilibrium, even when their dis-tortions assume the fantastic aspect of a dream. Guimard's woods (often pearwood) seem to have been shaped by his hands as if they were of metal and it was indeed in this material that he seems to have found his ideal medium. The famous gratings for the Métropolitain underground railway in Paris (1898-1904) gave birth to the term Style Métro. On doors, windows and stained glass Guimard wove ligaments of plants that climb and bend with extraordinary vigour. Curves are often described with the sharp precision of a working drawing and sometimes resemble the paraph of a signature. But this apparently free approach drew considerably on the past. Guimard himself did not hide his debt to the art of the Middle Ages, the spirit of which had been kept alive by Viollet-le-Duc and the Louis XV style and he also acknowledged the influence of the Belgian architects, Horta and van de Velde, on his early works in particular. Guimard's style nevertheless possesses a distinctly personal quality, steeped in reverie and prophecies. Today he emerges as the immediate precursor of Le Corbusier and modern architecture.

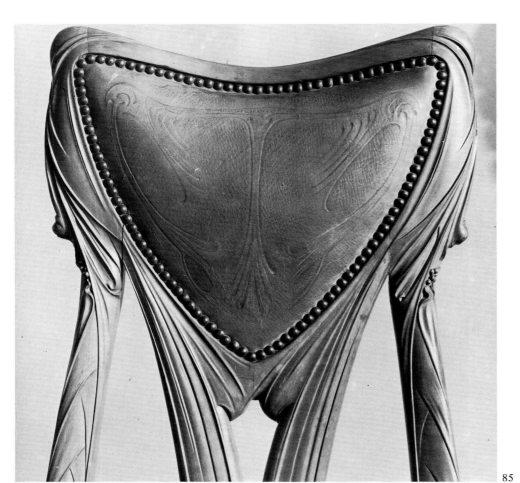

86

85

87

88

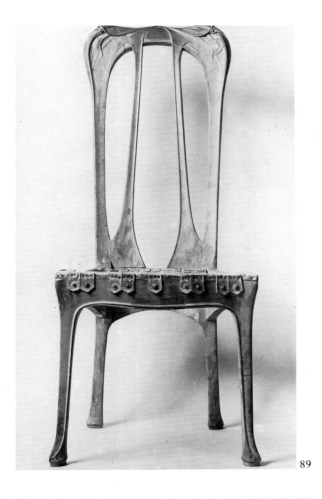

89

90

91

85 HECTOR GUIMARD Detail of pearwood chairback upholstered in leather. (Musée des Arts Décoratifs, Paris)

86 HECTOR GUIMARD Pearwood dressing-table. (Private Collection)

87 HECTOR GUIMARD Pearwood chair.

88 HECTOR GUIMARD Desk chair. (Galerie du Luxembourg, Paris)

89 HECTOR GUIMARD Chair upholstered with leather strips.

90 HECTOR GUIMARD Canapé-display case. (Galerie du Luxembourg, Paris)

91 HECTOR GUIMARD Armchair with accentuated curves. (Galerie du Luxembourg, Paris)

92

9

94

97

92-97 HECTOR GUIMARD Suite of furniture designed in 1907 comprising chairs, armchair, canapé, table, mantlepiece mirror and display cabinet. (Private Collection, Paris)

98

99

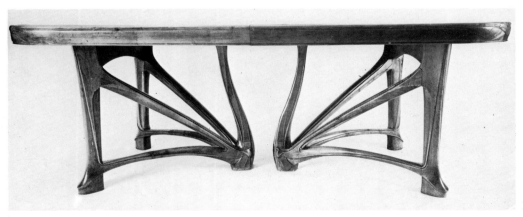

100

101

102

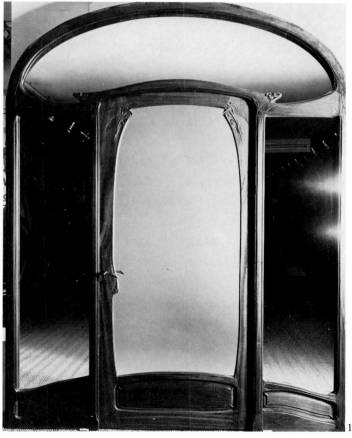

103

98 HECTOR GUIMARD   Cabinet. (Collection Félix Marcilhac, Paris)

99 HECTOR GUIMARD   Oak clock. (Musée des Arts Décoratifs, Paris)

100 HECTOR GUIMARD   Dining table. (Galerie du Luxembourg, Paris)

101 HECTOR GUIMARD   Desk and chair. (Galerie du Luxembourg, Paris)

102 HECTOR GUIMARD   Bedroom furniture. (Musée des Arts Décoratifs, Paris)

103 HECTOR GUIMARD   Wardrobe with mirror. (Galerie du Luxembourg, Paris)

SELMERSHEIM AND PLUMET

104

104 CHARLES PLUMET and TONY SELMERSHEIM Dressing-table, c.1900. (Hamburg Museum)

105-106 CHARLES PLUMET and TONY SELMERSHEIM Dining room suite and detail of the chairs. (This ensemble was originally displayed c.1897 in Joseph Durand-Ruel's apartment, rue de Rome)

105

106

SERRURIER, CHARPENTIER AND HOENTSCHEL

107

108

109

107 ALEXANDRE CHARPENTIER Large display cabinet. (Musée des Arts Décoratifs, Paris).

108 GUSTAVE SERRURIER-BOVY Three-tiered stand. (Galerie du Luxembourg, Paris)

109 ALEXANDRE CHARPENTIER Chairback in embossed leather on the theme of the convolvulus. (Mobilier National, Paris)

110 GEORGES HOENTSCHEL Dressing-table and chair next to a screen by Steiner. (Private Collection)

111 GEORGES HOENTSCHEL Algerian planewood armchair showing the influence of natural forms on artists at the beginning of the century. (Musée des Arts Décoratifs, Paris)

112 GEORGES HOENTSCHEL Large three-sided display cabinet. (Hamburg Museum)

110

111

112

113

114

115

113 Carved wooden chair in the Louis XV style. (Collection Manoukian, Paris)

114 CARLO BUGATTI Table, plant stand and guitar made c.1903 and inlaid with metal. (Private Collection)

115 ALPHONSE MUCHA Walnut stool upholstered in embossed leather. (Musée des Arts Décoratifs, Paris)

116 RUPERT CARABIN Detail of an armrest in the shape of a cat.

117 RUPERT CARABIN Desk in carved wood and wrought-iron in the form of a huge book supported by two female figures. (Private Collection, Paris)

RUPERT CARABIN

At the beginning of this century the furniture of Rupert Carabin (1862-1921) was unique. The interest in his work lay primarily in its sculpture rather than its qualities as an item of furniture. Carabin was born in Savern (Alsace) in 1862 and, after dabbling in a number of occupations, left for Paris in order to dedicate himself to sculpture. But he could not conceive of the statue as isolated from the rest of life. 'Stone,' he explained, 'is a cold, dead medium, but the artist who works in wood can integrate his figures into his furniture so that they participate in our daily existence.' His first work was a bookcase which, by incorporating a number of human figures, so contested classical conceptions that it was rejected by the Salon des Indépendants of 1890. But he was not discouraged and went on to create a multitude of women to support the weight of tables, chests and armchairs.

In spite of this anecdotal aspect of his work Carabin was an excellent sculptor who lavished great care on his woods, (obtained from the Auvergne), maturing them for eight years during which time they were impregnated with oils in the course of interminable massages designed to create a gloss and to 'give them life'. A Pygmalion of modern times, Carabin aimed to endow his figurines with life and movement and achieved this, for example, with his statue of Loïe Fuller.

116

117

118

11

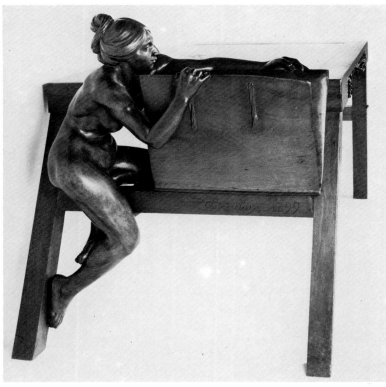

120

12

118 RUPERT CARABIN Carved pearwood bookcase with the figure of Wisdom, a star on her forehead, holding out her hand to a woman. On top of the case are two busts, one by Sarah Bernhardt and the other by Joseph Bernard. (Galerie du Luxembourg, Paris)

119 RUPERT CARABIN The figure of Loïe Fuller in glazed ceramic.

120 RUPERT CARABIN Work bench with a female figure opening a port-folio.

121 RUPERT CARABIN Chest 'à la pieuvre' in carved walnut. (Galerie du Luxembourg, Paris)

122 RUPERT CARABIN Femme Chauve-souris in bronze, the bat-woman's wings forming a receptacle. (Collection Félix Marcilhac, Paris)

123

123 **RUPERT CARABIN** Corner cupboard of carved oak and wrought-iron. (Musée de l'École de Nancy)

COMPARATIVE SURVEY

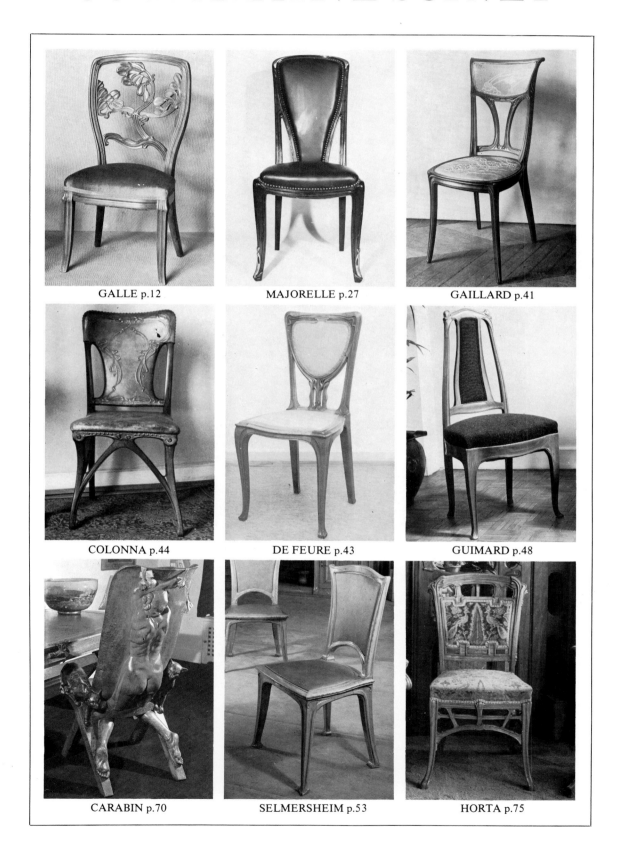

GALLE p.12

MAJORELLE p.27

GAILLARD p.41

COLONNA p.44

DE FEURE p.43

GUIMARD p.48

CARABIN p.70

SELMERSHEIM p.53

HORTA p.75

MAJORELLE p.30   GAILLARD p.42   GUIMARD p.50

HOENTSCHEL p.55   CHARPENTIER p.54   CARABIN p.58

GALLE p.20   MAJORELLE p.33   GUIMARD p.49

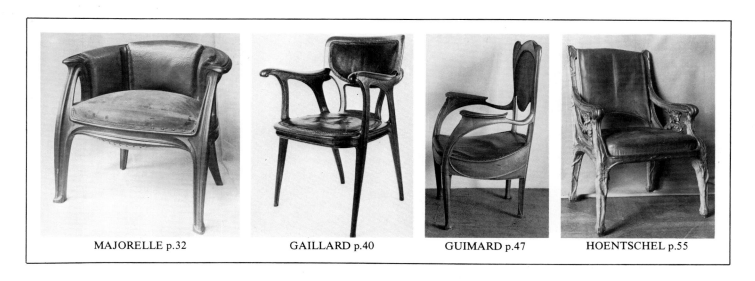

MAJORELLE p.32   GAILLARD p.40   GUIMARD p.47   HOENTSCHEL p.55

GALLE p.18   GAILLARD p.39   COLONNA p.44

GUIMARD p.50   SELMERSHEIM p.53   CARABIN p.57

GALLE p.15   MAJORELLE p.23   GAILLARD p.40   HORTA p.73

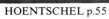

GAILLARD p.42

HOENTSCHEL p.55

VALLIN p.69

GRUBER p.36

GUIMARD p.51

GALLE p.18

VALLIN p.34

GRUBER p.37

124 **EMILE GALLE** Console, *Les Parfums d'Autrefois*, (Musée de l'Ecole de Nancy)

125 EMILE GALLE Bed, *Aube et Crépuscule* with magnificent marquetry work. (Musée de l'Ecole de Nancy)

126 LOUIS MAJORELLE Piano with marquetry work by Emile Gallé. (Musée de l'Ecole de Nancy)

127 LOUIS MAJORELLE Symbolic console based on designs by Victor Prouvé and signed 'Nancy 1893'. (Collection Jean-Claude Brugnot)

128 EUGENE VALLIN Unusual ensemble of desk and chair and large piece comprising display cabinet, bench seat, console and cupboard. (Musée de l'Ecole de Nancy)

129 RUPERT CARABIN Desk and chair, the back of which is supported by a nymph acting as a buttress who holds in her hands the lengths of silk attached to the headrest. (Private Collection, Paris)

130 Mahogany cabinet made in Carlisle c.1898. The bronze ornamentation and enamel plaques are attributed to Mucha. (Private Collection)

131 CHARLES RENNIE MACKINTOSH Cabinet of dark stained wood with inlaid ivory and mother-of-pearl and twin ovals of mauve glass. The central decorative panel is of leaded green, white and mirror glass set in zinc in the form of a stylised roseball.

126

127

128

129

130

131

EUROPEAN ART NOUVEAU OUTSIDE FRANCE

Belgium

A comprehensive view of Art Nouveau would be incomplete without recognition of the important role of those artists outside France who heralded the movement before it appeared in Nancy and Paris. Social and artistic currents born in England towards the middle of the nineteenth century spread to the continent, initially to Belgium, from 1880 onwards. Brussels became 'a cross-roads for ideas, a centre for exalted exchanges'. Under the influence of such writers as Maurice Maeterlinck, Max Elskamp, Camille Lemonnier and Emile Verhaeren, its intellectual life intensified and acquired an international dimension. The revue *L'Art Moderne*, founded in 1881, took up the theories of William Morris who stated that art that possessed no social aim was a contemptible luxury. From this spirit of social and artistic renewal several movements came into being: Le Cercle des Vingt (1884),

l'Art Indépendant (Anvers 1887), La Libre Esthétique (1899). Periodicals and associations played a major role in the growth of Symbolism and Naturalism as it spread to embrace all modes of expression.

Two architects, Paul Hankar and, more importantly, Victor Horta were the real creators of Belgian Art Nouveau. In particular, the conservatories at Laeken, designed and constructed by Horta for Leopold II, are a revelation of the resourcefulness of iron. This material, previously reserved for exhibition pavilions, was introduced by Horta into the architecture of the private house. One of the masterpieces of the genre was the house built in Brussels from 1892 for the engineer, Emile Tassel.

132 **VICTOR HORTA** One of the rooms in the Musée Horta in Brussels.

132

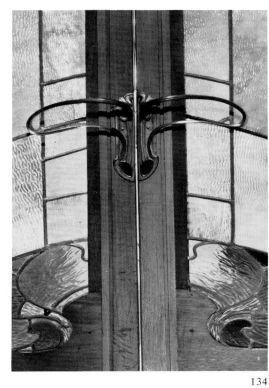

133

134

135

136

137

138

139

133-135 VICTOR HORTA Selection of locks and door handles showing the importance Horta attached to the smallest detail.

136 VICTOR HORTA The novel use of wide doorways and windows and open stairwells to allow light to flood the room.

137 VICTOR HORTA A corner of the dining-room in the Hotel Solvay, avenue Louise, Brussels, designed in 1895.

138 VICTOR HORTA Chair and armchair from the Hotel Solvay.

139 VICTOR HORTA Wrought-iron banister. (Musée Horta, Brussels)

140 VICTOR HORTA Dining-room furniture from the Hotel Solvay.

140

142

141 HENRY VAN DE VELDE Bench seat incorporating a bookcase.

142-143 HENRY VAN DE VELDE Two views of a small cabinet with the top open and closed.

144 HENRY VAN DE VELDE Table and chest of drawers from van de Velde's house in Weimer. (Collection Knut Günther)

141

144

143

Germany

Art Nouveau came belatedly to Germany, and was of a less uniform nature than in France and England. Munich, Darmstadt, Berlin and Pforzheim were the main centres where the new stylistic tendencies appeared, in one form or another.

Two revues, *Pan* (founded in Berlin by the art historian Julius Meier-Graefe, who had close links with the Art Nouveau movement in Paris) and, in particular, *Jugend* (Munich 1896) defended the floral style and symbolism. Jugendstil, the generic term for German Art Nouveau, was derived from the name of *Jugend*, the official organ of the young artists.

The most ardent protagonists of Jugendstil were not the specialists but intellectuals and artists. The naturalist, Hermann Obrist (1862-1927) transposed the supple structures of plants into plastic forms. The line of his furniture is nevertheless robust and often has a gnarled appearance. He was also interested in sculpture, ceramics and embroidery — the embroidery art workshop that he opened in Florence in 1892 was moved to Munich in 1894. The painter Otto Eckmann (1865-1902) promoted the arabesque in his furniture, as in his wallpapers and tapestries, which also possessed a grace derived from Japanese art. August Endell (1871-1925), who was very influenced by Obrist, created furniture, fabrics and jewellery but was particularly famous for his Elvira workshops, a masterpiece of Germanic lyricism which has since been demolished. Richard Riemerschmid (1868-1957), one of the founders of the Vereinigten Werkstätten für Kunst in Handwerk, (United Workshops for Art in Craftswork) adopted a more sober and functional line and tried to adapt it to industrial production. In 1900, he exhibited in Paris with Bruno Paul and Bernhard Pankok (1872-1943). Alongside the floral fantasies, no longer in the ascendancy, a constructive tendency began to appear. It was confirmed by the work of Peter Behrens (1868-1940), the architect, painter, decorator and illustrator. After his arrival in Darmstadt, where he joined the artists of the Mathildenhohe, an avant-garde group, Behrens committed himself once and for all to the path towards abstraction.

The Jugendstil, at Darmstadt, assumed a character that was very far removed from floral art. Several foreign artists, including the Englishmen, Ashbee and Baillie Scott and the Belgian, van de Velde, were summoned to assist in the decoration of the New Palace. The Grand Duke of Hesse also commissioned the Austrian Joseph-Maria Olbrich as architect of the Mathildenhohe, near Darmstadt. A pupil of Otto Wagner (1841-1918), who strictly advocated the primacy of structure over decoration, Olbrich introduced the simple linear style of Austria into Germany. His influence was critical for after the Turin Exhibition of 1902, the Germans abandoned the Jugend floral style and by 1904, in Saint-Louis, a critic could affirm that 'the transgressions of the Jugendstil have been vanquished.'

145

146

145 HERMANN OBRIST Table, c.1902. (Collection Knut Günther)

146 HERMANN OBRIST Table whose legs are joined to a central base, c.1898. (Private Collection, Bavaria)

Austria

The term Secessionstil is derived from a group of Austrian avant-garde painters, sculptors and decorators known as the Wiener Secession. Their first exhibition was held in March 1898 in a rather daring building specially designed for the purpose. But it is doubtful to what extent Secessionstil was a part of Art Nouveau. In many ways it was its antithesis, rejecting asymmetrical forms and the floral elements of Jugendstil. Though it took up the theories of Otto Wagner — that only the beautiful can be useful and that it was necessary to be simple and make an open display of the construction and the materials — it ignored naturalism and presented itself from the start as an autonomous contemporary style. A number of artists were ranged around Gustav Klimt, who directed the movement: Josef Hoffmann (1870-1956), the painter and architect, Joseph-Maria Olbrich (1867-1908) and Adolph Loos (1870-1933) were amongst the most influential.

The works of Hoffmann, known as Quadratl Hoffmann, were the product of a synthesis of the theories of Otto Wagner and aesthetics of the Scot, Mackintosh: rectilinear furniture, geometric designs based on the rectangle and the square, black and white ornamentations of ivory, ebony and silver. In 1903, Hoffmann founded, with Koloman Moser and Carl Otto Czeschka, the Wiener Werkstätte organisation which was of decisive importance to the evolution of the group. From 1905 to 1911 Hoffmann built the Palais Stoclet in Brussels, commissioned by a rich patron with the help of Klimt who contributed the mural mosaics. The result was a combination of severe architecture and a decor of oriental sumptuosity.

147 BERNHARD PANKOK Double bed made up of two single section, 90 centimetres wide which can be used separately. Built of cherrywood with inlays of other woods it was designed by Pankok for his own use on the occasion of his marriage. (Regional Museum, Wurtemburg)

148 BERNHARD PANKOK Solid German oak canapé from Obrist's house, 1899. (Vereinigte Werkstätten, Munich)

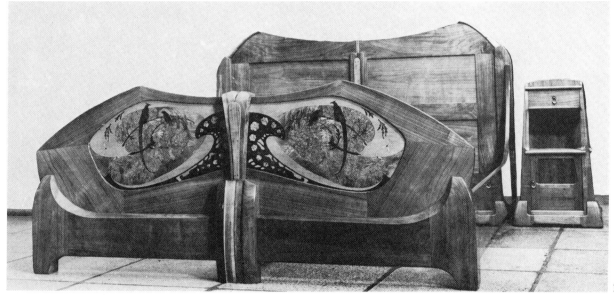

147

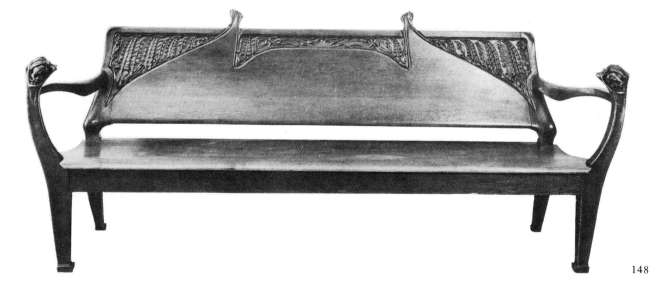

148

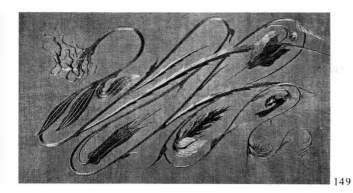

149 HERMANN OBRIST *Violettes des Alpes*, a wall-hanging in gold silk on a blue-green woollen background, made c.1895 by Berthe Ruchet.

150 Meissen porcelain statuette, (Collection Andrée Vyncke)

151 JOSEF HOFFMANN Small oak desk. (Österreichisches Museum der bildenden Künste)

152 JOSEPH OLBRICH Grand piano in black polished wood. (Regional Museum, Hesse)

153 Dining room in the Steffery Castle.

Great Britain

In England, the first signs of an artistic revival appeared around the middle of the nineteenth century. Reacting against the ugliness of the Industrial Arts displayed in London at the Great Exhibitions of 1851 and 1862, John Ruskin, the art historian and William Morris, the painter, poet and decorator raised the standard of revolt. They extolled the virtues of manual labour, the nobility of the craftsman, the oneness of all the arts and the need to create a social art — 'for the people and by the people'. Young artists, painters, architects and decorators were fired with enthusiasm by their theories. Philip Webb (1831-1915) and Richard Norman Shaw (1831-1912) recreated private architecture in accordance with the new concepts of the Domestic Revival. The best Pre-Raphaelite painters, Dante-Gabriel Rossetti (1828-1882), Edward Burne-Jones (1833-1898) and Ford Madox Brown (1821-1893) joined Morris and contributed towards the social and aesthetic revolution. Their aim was to produce works of applied art of an artistic character and at low prices.

It seems contradictory that this generation, which repudiated the Academy, historicism, pastiche and the Victorian passion for carpets and hangings, should draw inspiration from mediaeval art, the Quattrocento (Botticelli in particular) and the Celtic tradition. But nostalgia for the past, difficult to eradicate, was strengthened by two modernist currents, Symbolism and Naturalism. And from that symbiosis English Art Nouveau was born.

The foundation in 1888 of the Arts and Crafts Exhibition Society increased the influence of Morris' reforms. Arthur Heygate Mackmurdo was a key personality of this movement. The frontispiece of *Wren's City Churches* (a work dedicated to the English Baroque of Christopher Wren) affirmed, in 1883, the new stylistic tendencies: the floral theme, undulating lines and a Japanese-influenced graphism. Mackmurdo

154

155

154 CHARLES RENNIE MACKINTOSH Painted oak chair, c.1901.

155 PHILIP WEBB Cabinet painted on the theme of St. George.

156

57

156 CHARLES RENNIE MACKINTOSH Design for a dining-room, 1901.

157 WALTER CRANE Illustration.

created not only fabrics, wallpapers and jewellery, but furniture, characterised by the play of horizontal and vertical lines which was architectural rather than naturalistic in conception. Charles Annesley Voysey tended towards an even more simplified and rigorous approach, notably in certain pieces of furniture embellished by no more than the metallic motifs that surround their locks. He also designed fabrics and wallpapers, drawing his decorative themes from a repertoire of animals and plants.

The creations of Christopher Dresser (1834-1904) and Charles Robert Ashbee (1863-1942) were derived from the same aesthetic of simplification based on the line, that prefigured contemporary tendencies. Ashbee and Mackhay Hugh Baillie Scott (1865-1945) were summoned to Germany in 1898 for the decoration of the Darmstadt Palace and made a considerable contribution towards the spreading of English taste throughout the continent, with the exception of France. In return, French Art Nouveau hardly influenced the English movement at all, except through the work of Eugène Grasset, who was most unjustly disregarded in his own country.

The designer Walter Crane (1845-1915) fully exploited the expressive potential of lines and curves, while tempering his asymmetrical forms with a judicious control. In addition to his illustrations (for *Flora's Feast* and numerous other children's books) his prolific talent unleashed on to paper and fabrics a wealth of stylised flowerings.

The same spirit of reform animated the Scottish architect, Charles Rennie Mackintosh, the founder with Herbert MacNair and the sisters Margaret and Frances Macdonald, of the Glasgow group. The concepts upheld by this group were clearly defined: functional design, perfect workmanship and decorative charm. The languid playfulness of the curve is contained within the rigid, vertical structure of their furniture. Many items were produced in lacquered woods in white, and other clear, light colours, frequently enhanced with incrustations of precious materials, such as mother-of-pearl, enamel, ivory or coloured glass, bearing stylised motifs of symbolist inspiration. The long, curved silhouette of the 'lady with the rose' was a popular ornamental theme for these artists. The refined and very personal nature of their sensibility was reflected in their use of the Art Nouveau colours of pale pink, mauve, soft greens and pearl grey. 'In Glasgow,' noted the art critic Julius Meier-Graefe, 'English art is no longer hermaphroditic, it has passed into the realm of the woman.' The group held successful exhibitions in Vienna (1900), Dresden (1901) and Turin (1902). Acting as a synthesis of fantasy and rationalism, it exerted a decisive influence on German and Austrian artists. But this increasingly precious approach was difficult to reconcile with the large scale production necessary if the original aim, that of beauty within the reach of all, were to be realised.

15

16

158

158 ARTHUR HEYGATE MACKMURDO Oak writing desk.

159 WILLIAM MORRIS Wallpaper entitled *Burnets*.

160 WILLIAM MORRIS Reversible fabric of silk and wool.

161 Scandinavian Art Nouveau furniture.

162 HVITTRASK Furniture and decor.

163 Mahogany display cabinet, c.1901.

161

162

163

WALL DECORATION

FABRICS

The Art Nouveau style did not bring about a revolution in the style of fabrics, nor in the techniques of production, which were already highly advanced. It was rather a period of transition between the predominantly sombre compositions of the late nineteenth century and the explosions of colour inspired by the Ballets Russes, which set the tone for the 1925 Exhibition of Decorative Arts. Colours tended to be softer and often in pastel shades, perhaps due to the development of improved chemical processes. It was also an era in which the official painters, such as Puvis de Chavannes, softened their darker tones and stylised form and line. This stylisation, often sacrificed by the furniture maker in favour of luxurious vegetation sculpted in wood, was more strictly observed by designers of fabrics. For they were obliged to work in only two dimensions, in the knowledge that the arabesques they composed would be juxtaposed and repeated in a recurring pattern.

164-165 CHARLES FRIDRICH *Les Ombelles and Les Glycines* 1901.

164

165

166

167

168

169

166 KARBOWSKY Lampas fabric.

167 MAURICE DUFRENE Orange damask. (Collection Tassinari and Chatel)

168 *Les Clematites*. (Musée de l'Ecole de Nancy)

169 KARBOWSKY Lampas fabric with cream and yellow motifs, 1903. (Collection Tassinari and Chatel)

170

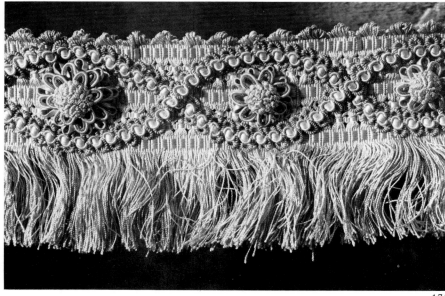

171

172

170-172 Selection of Art Nouveau trimmings. (Collection La Passementerie nouvelle)

WALLPAPER

The evolution of wallpaper and fabrics has traditionally been parallel, since the role of wallpaper was to provide an economic substitute for the latter. New developments have since allowed wallpaper to imitate lacquer, wood and practically all the traditional materials.

In 1900, wallpaper was still following the example set by fabrics. Wallpaper designers, inspired by nature, inevitably used the flower as a decorative motif, though in a stylised and fanciful manner. In their desire to tackle all the disciplines, men such as Hector Guimard and Victor Bourgeois, created numerous sketches featuring a multitude of irises, cyclamens, lilies of the valley, cow-parsley, waterlilies, clematis and plane trees and occasionally, human figures amongst the vegetation. But no sooner had this tendency asserted itself than it began to give way to the more stylised Art Deco style.

173 VICTOR BOURGEOIS Wallpaper, 1901.

174-175 BAEYENS Designs for wallpapers, c.1900.

173

174

175

176

177

176-177 VICTOR BOURGEOIS Wallpapers, 1901. (Musée des Arts
Décoratifs, Paris)

TAPESTRY

In France tapestry remained firmly linked to the pictorial tradition and did not seek, as in the Nordic countries, to create a new form of expression. The Gobelin workshop commissioned cartoons from the fashionable artists of the day, which were subsequently reproduced with a disconcerting exactitude. Whether in the modelling, shading or choice of half-tints, the craftsman was forbidden to make any omission or personal interpretation. The chivalrous scenes of Jules Chéret (1836-1933) transport us back, in a whirl of elegant dresses to the light, frothy atmosphere of the Belle Epoque. Georges Rochegrosse (1859-1939) does not possess that seductive charm. His allegories still, as then, create a heavy ponderous impression. The compositions of Adolphe Willette (1857-1926), however, are charged with a poetic gracefulness and psychological penetration that make him flatteringly akin to Watteau.

178 BERONNEAU *Salomé.*

179 ROCHEGROSSE *La France distribuant ses bienfaits aux peuples d'Afrique et d'Asie.*

180 WEBER *La Belle au Bois dormant.*

181 ADOLPHE WILLETTE *Salut à Paris.*

182 JULES CHERET *L'Hiver.* (Mobilier National, Paris)

178

179

89

180

181

182

STAINED GLASS

Stained glass played an important role in decoration at the beginning of this century. Those artists who found inspiration for their furniture, fabrics and wallpapers in landscapes, flowers and greenery discovered in stained glass a surface that was free, transparent and luminous. Henceforth there was scarcely a stairway, winter garden, veranda or interior door where the light was not filtered through bouquets of irises, fields of thistles or garlands of flowers. The best of these stained glass windows, such as those signed by Grüber, Grasset or Guimard, were executed in the traditional manner, whereby motifs were outlined by a tracery of lead. Others consisted simply of regular series of small panes of painted or enamelled glass. The current fashion for wide expanses of glass has largely done away with the stained glass window. Our contemporaries prefer the sight of a real tree or small corner of greenery to that of a painted garden brought to life by the rays of the sun.

183 Painted and enamelled stained glass window. (Private Collection)

184 HECTOR GUIMARD Piece of stained glass. (Galerie du Luxembourg, Paris)

185 JACQUES GRUBER Flowers and birds.

183

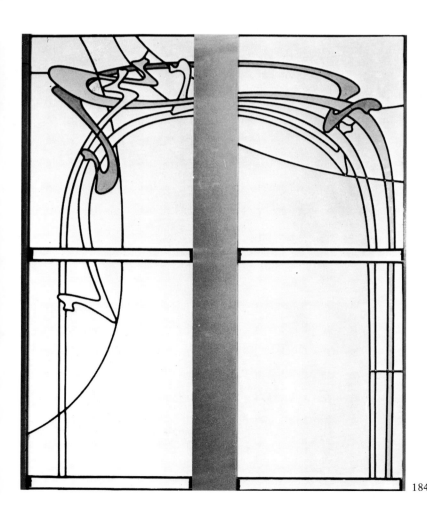

184

185

186

188

187

186 JACQUES GRUBER Stained glass window designed in 1905 for a house in Nancy.

187 EUGENE GRASSET Stained glass window. (Musée des Arts Décoratifs, Paris)

188 HECTOR GUIMARD Stained glass in a stair-well on the rue La Fontaine, Paris.

APPLIED ARTS
CERAMICS

The ceramic revival of the late nineteenth century was no less spectacular than its counterpart in the field of glassware. The first signs of a renaissance appeared in the 1850s when the growing number of small workshops effected a break between industry, with its fixed routines and the individual artist in search of new means of expression. The triumph of individualism was completed within a few years, when the name of the workshop or manufacturer gave way to that of the craftsman. Even pieces executed at Limoges or Sèvres were often designated by the name of the ceramist. The feverish creativity of these potters can be traced back to several origins: the veneration of manual work and craftsmanship by Ruskin and Morris, a passionate interest in chemistry brought about by scientific developments and the influence of the ancient arts of China and Japan. The all too seductive charms of decorated porcelain were rejected in favour of monochromes, rougher materials such as stoneware and dense 'grand feu' (high temperature fired) glazes impregnated with the marks left by intense heat.

Théodore Deck (1823-1891) can be considered as the pioneer of the new ceramics. His early works all refer to past styles: Italian majolica, Oriental pottery, Hispano-Moresque earthenware, interpreted with a distinctive personal technique. From around 1880 Deck's production centred around Chinese flambé earthenware and imitations of the celadons and glazed biscuitware of the Sung and Ming dynasties.

Ernest Chaplet (1835-1909) started in 1848 as an apprentice in decoration work with the Sèvres workshops. In the early 1870s, Chaplet perfected a new process, known as 'barbotine' – virtually a form of painting – that used coloured clays thinned with water. Barbotine became the medium of miniature painting and subjects depicted in precise detail but quickly fell into disrepute. Today, however, it is once again sought out by the collector.

In 1875, Chaplet joined the Haviland-Auteuil workshop. The engraver Bracquemond, an enthusiast of the art of the Far East, was artistic director there and he introduced Chaplet to the beautiful flambé vases of China. They were nothing short of a revelation to him and from then on, Chaplet devoted himself to experimentation with strongly fired stoneware. In collaboration with Albert Dammouse and Hexamer, Chaplet created items that were both simple and robust, in brown earthenware, decorated with polychrome glazes and finished in gold, depicting fruit, flowers and naturalistic scenes. He was also interested in porcelain and rediscovered the secret of the 'sang-de-boeuf' glazings of the Chinese masters, which he always refused to divulge. In 1887, he gave up his workshop to Auguste Delaherche and settled in Choisy-le-Roi, where he devoted himself to experiments

of personal interest. It was a period of simplification, of superb flambé effects produced by the atmosphere of the kiln. In 1904, Chaplet, having gone blind, surrendered the direction of his workshop to his son-in-law, Emile Lenoble. A number of Chaplet's pieces bear the mark 'au rosaire', an allusion to the artist's name which is similar in meaning to the word 'rosaire.'

Albert Dammouse (1848-1926) was the son of a sculptor of the Sèvres workshop and was himself a painter and sculptor. He was an excellent technician who studied all the methods of porcelain decoration and perfected a complex procedure involving the application of coloured pastes, overlaid with glaze. In 1882, Haviland invited him to work with Chaplet in the manufacture of 'decorated stoneware'. Dammouse was immediately captivated by this material and the decorative

189 Freize from a delicatessen in Nancy (demolished in 1964). (Musée de l'Ecole de Nancy)

sobriety of his first works reflects the influence of Japanese monochrome. As his style evolved the surfaces of his vases were discreetly brought to life with flowers, sea-plants and foliage fired with polychrome glazes.

Auguste Delaherche (1857-1940) was born into a family of potters at Beauvaisis, not far from Savignies, a busy centre of ceramic production in past centuries. Like Chaplet, he was attracted to stoneware and actually took over Chaplet's workshop in the rue Blomet in 1887. His first works conformed to the fashion for naturalistic decoration engraved onto the glazed surface. Otherwise it was his forms that were inspired by nature; the melon, gourd or corolla, their glazes poured on, creating flambés and opalescent, iridescent effects. Other items were influenced by the arts of Persia, China and Japan. Removing, little by little, any suggestion of figuration from his work, Delaherche eventually arrived at the simplified style of the Chinese potters of the Tang and Sung periods. This search for purity led him to his final phase of white porcelain, initially flambéd in gold and aventurine, then monochrome in imitation of the Chinese Whites, in the manner of which it was also engraved and perforated.

Pierre-Adrien Dalpayrat (1844-1910), born at Limoges, learnt the craft of ceramics at a very early age. After practising as a master potter in Bordeaux, Toulouse, Limoges and Monte-Carlo, Dalpayrat settled in 1889 at Bourg-le-Reine and specialised in flambé stoneware, while still maintaining an interest in china and porcelain. His forms were simple and frequently of Japanese inspiration, while the animals, figures and plants that decorated his cups and vases provided scope for his imagination. Always receptive to new processes, he perfected a glaze known as 'Dalpayrat Red', based on copper. He also produced, in association with Adèle Lesbros and Voisin, a series of cheaply priced stoneware.

Alexandre Bigot (1862-1927) was a ceramist whose career was also determined by the stoneware of the Far East. A Doctor of Science and Professor of Physics and Chemistry at the Ecole Alsacienne, Bigot initially devoted himself to technical research concerning clays and glazes and eventually settled at Mer (Loir-et-Cher). In 1894 his first exhibition revealed to the public his restrained creations, simple forms embellished with matt glazes in tones of yellow, brown and green. After winning the Grand Prix at the 1900 Exhibition he became increasingly interested in both exterior and interior architectural decoration, working with such sculptors as Emile Bourdelle and Fix-Masseau.

Edmond Lachenal, born in 1865, was a painter, sculptor and ceramist. He was trained by Théodore Deck and his first earthenware was inspired by the rich decoration of Isnik. Lachenal was an avid experimentalist and perfected a process of metallo-ceramic electrolysis using hydroflouric acid to obtain 'glossy-matt' effects. He was alternately influenced by Art Nouveau and the Far East. His work consists of robust stoneware made from the highest quality materials enriched with velvety-toned glazes or discreetly painted decorations, of earthenware embellished with gold and above all, fine ceramic sculptures. He also transposed the work of his artistic friends into stoneware: Rodin, Agnès de Fourmerie, Dejean and Saint-Marceaux. His son, Raoul (1885-1956) succeeded to his workshop.

L'Ecole de Saint-Amand-en-Puisaye

Jean Carriès (1855-1894), born at Lyon, used both his forceful personality and the fruits of his research to give a new impetus to the art of stoneware. It was as a thirty-three year old sculptor that Carriès developed a passion for this material which he called the 'king of porcelains' and set out to reinstate its expressive power. His arrival at Saint-Amand-en-Puisaye in 1888 overturned all the notions of the Nivernais potters. He installed himself in the Manor of Montriveau, whence vases of a robust, refined simplicity began to appear, along with other monochrome items of a rough appearance, inspired by ancient Japanese pottery. His production can be divided, on a somewhat arbitrary basis, into three categories: the 'grey family', produced with kiln ashes, the 'cinder family', decorated with grey-blue glazes produced with wood cinders and the 'wax family', featuring a feldspar glaze of waxy appearance, white or shaded with brown. But the sculptures constitute the most distinctive feature of Carriès' production, consisting of masks, monsters, animals (in particular, some strange frogs with rabbit ears) and tormented forms which create a disturbing effect that no doubt exteriorised the imaginings of their creator. This unexpected element in his work prefigured the Surrealist movement.

A group of ceramists formed around Jean Carriès, from which the Ecole de Saint-Amand-en-Puisaye emerged. 'Clay is good', said Carriès, 'full of silica, but with little iron and no porous elements. The raw material is everything, or virtually everything.'

Georges Hoentschel (1855-1915) was a decorator, who turned to ceramics as a new form of expression. At first he was strongly influenced by the works of Carriès and by Japanese art, but he quickly broke free and his work became saturated, sometimes to a fault, with the flora of Art Nouveau. One outcome of his eclectic tastes was to mount his vases with chased bronze, treated with a patina, in the eighteenth–century manner. He also produced a number of

190 EMILE GALLE Porcelain bowl. (Private Collection)

larger items, in particular, a bath for the Comtesse de Ganay.

Paul Jeanneney (1861-1920), a man of refined tastes and collector of Far-Eastern ceramics, began to interest himself in the art of stoneware. Having installed himself at Saint-Amand-en-Puisaye, where he was to remain until his death, Jeanneney took inspiration from the art of the Far East and from the techniques of his colleague. His vases, which derive from Chinese flambé stoneware and Japanese 'trompe-l'oeil' effects (sections of bamboo, double gourds) are of the finest materials, enriched with thick, flowing applications of glossy and matt glazes of subdued tones.

Emile Grittel (1870-1953), painter and sculptor, also turned to ceramics through the influence of Carriès. Influenced by Japanese art, he made a lighter variety of stoneware decorated with matt glazes that were usually dark and monochrome and occasionally heightened with touches of gold.

Armand and Eugène Lion, from a family of potters at Saint-Amand-en-Puisaye and specialists in utilitarian stoneware, were influenced by Carriès and took up 'artistic stoneware'. Other Japanese influenced craftsmen of the same school were the Abbé Pierre Pacton (1856-1938), Jean Pointu (1843-1925) and Théo Perrot. They all created distinctly 'personalised' works which are now avidly sought out by the contemporary collector.

After 1900 the disciples of the Japanese and Modern styles were succeeded by a new generation. Methey, Decoeur, Lenoble and many others gave, by means of their research and creativity, a new impetus to ceramics.

André Methey (1871-1920) left his native Côte d'Or at the age of 15 to learn the craft of the potter in Paris. His aim was to promote colour above all else. He had a great admiration for Arabic and Persian ceramics and endeavoured to recreate the same rich glazes. In 1903 he settled in Asnières and began to experiment with the clays of the Ile-de-France. His pieces were coated with a white tin glaze and were designed to show off the decorations produced by his friends, the painters, Georges Rouault, Edouard Vuillard, Maurice Denis, Odilon Redon and Maurice de Vlaminck. In 1907, at the Salon d'Automne, Methey exhibited 100 splendid items of glazed earthenware, explosions of pure colour that rallied to the fanfare of the Fauves. His compositions were at first geometric in style, but elements of flora and fauna were gradually introduced. 'It is most important; he said, 'that things should change.'

Emile Lenoble (1875-1940), son-in-law of Ernest Chaplet, was drawn towards stoneware decoration, for which he adopted several techniques. His painted decorations were applied in a free style, sober yet never dry, while his engraved decorations were either made straight on to the basic material or inscribed into the glaze. His incrustations of coloured clay recall the earthenware of Orron. His geometric motifs, often of Greek inspiration, of spirals, coils or herring-bone patterns, elaborated on the handle or shoulder of the vase, follow clear symmetrical rhythms. Nor did Lenoble escape the influence of the Far East and of Korean, Japanese and Chinese potteries of the Tang or Sung dynasties in particular.

Emile Decoeur (1878-1953) was at first influenced by Lachenal, but his personality was of a sort that quickly rebelled against influence. Having settled in at Fontenay-aux-

Roses, Decoeur turned his attention to stoneware and highly-fired porcelains. After the tortured themes of Art Nouveau – its 'errors of youth' – his work assumed a character of its own, consisting of a rare sense of balance between the volume, the basic material and the glaze.

Fernand Rumèbe (1875-1952) learnt the techniques of ceramics with Emile Decoeur. His works, small in number and reserved for a few friends, reflect the accumulated memories of his travels to the countries of the Mediterranean and the Orient. Mussulman ceramics, Khmer temples and Oriental carpets were a source of inspiration for his sober, virtually abstract, motifs which are emphasised by the richness of the glazes.

Etienne Moreau-Nelaton (1859-1917) was a painter, writer and collector who also turned to pottery, following the example of his mother, Camille Moreau-Nelaton, herself a ceramist. He had a particular talent for decoration, drawing from the repertoire of Art Nouveau.

Félix Massoul (1872-1938), initially a painter, applied the same painterly skills to his glazes. His art was founded on a solid knowledge of techniques, both archaeological and modern. He studied all aspects of the art of ceramics, from Egyptian ceramics to Gallo-Roman pottery, Hispano-Moresque earthenware to the delicate creations of the eighteenth century. Massoul's creations in white earthenware are covered in sumptuous glazes frequently applied in accordance with geometric design schemes, through which nude forms occasionally emerge from the natural under-surface.

Clément Massier (1845-1917) established himself at Vallauris in 1872, where he worked with two members of his family, Delphin and Jérome. It was in their workshop that Lucien Lévy-Dhurmer, the painter of an Art Nouveau style feminine charm, produced some surprising earthenware of Oriental inspiration with a gleaming metallic finish. Two specific aspects of the Massiers' approach contributed to

191 JEAN CARRIES Frog with rabbit ears. (Private Collection)

their success; the lustre that they produced was evocative of Hispano-Moresque earthenware, yet it also emanated a rich green-violet glow that was very much their own. The form and the ornamental motifs were inspired either by the animated rhythms of Art Nouveau, or the rigorous volumes and muted tones of antique models.

The list of honours would be incomplete without the inclusion of Emile Gallé, whose first incursion into the decorative arts was in the field of ceramics.

Following the fruitless efforts of the Sèvres workshops to effect a re-flowering of the art of porcelain, Bing, founder of the Galerie Art Nouveau, decided to tackle the problem. He wanted to restore 'grand feu' porcelains, with decorated glazings, to the important position they had enjoyed in China before the Ts'ing era and in Japan. This difficult enterprise drew heavily on the technical procedures employed by the Royal Workshops of Copenhagen and the famous Danish firm of Bing and Gröndahl, under the direction of the painter, Willumsen. The experimental items that emerged from this new approach are not without interest. Edward Colonna and, above all, Georges de Feure, who brought versatility and brio to Art Nouveau, produced items of an exquisite refinement.

Taxile Doat (1851-1938) initially followed a course in design at the Ecole Adrien-Dubouché in Limoges. Afterwards, he went to Paris, and in 1877 was working in the Sèvres workshops. The publication of a work entitled *Grand Feu Ceramics* provoked considerable interest in the United States and Doat was invited to Saint-Louis to teach the art of ceramics at the Univeristy, where he remained until 1914.

192 **AUGUSTE DELAHERCHE** Large bowl. (Collection Alain Lesieutre, Paris)

193

194

193-194 ALEXANDRE BIGOT Animals. (Collection Alain Lesieutre, Paris)

195 LOUIS MAJORELLE Vase. (Collection Alain Lesieutre, Paris)

196 JEAN RINGEL D'ILLZACH Grotesque head. (Collection S. Dali)

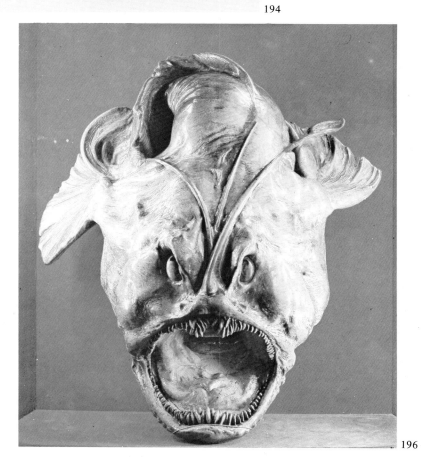

195

196

197

19

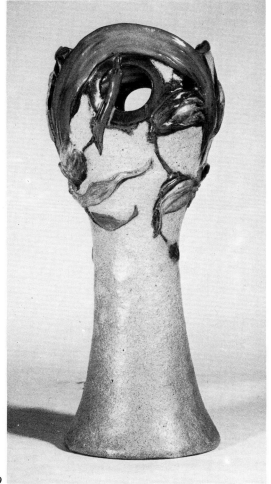

199

200

20

197 PIERRE ADRIEN DALPAYRAT and ADELE LESBROS Vase with panthers.

198 PAUL JEANNENEY Ceramic vase.

199 ROBOLSTEIN Ceramic vase. (Collection Félix Marcilhac, Paris)

200 PIERRE ADRIEN DALPAYRAT Ceramic gourd.

201 DELPHIN MASSIER Vase made at Vallauris.

203

02

202 JEAN CARRIES Mask of enamelled stoneware.

203 DEGRANGE Painted terra cotta flower pot. (Collection Félix Marcilhac, Paris)

204 FERNAND RUMEBE Ceramic plate.

205 FELIX MASSOUL Crackled ceramic bowl.

05

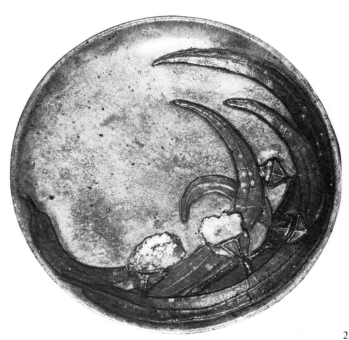

204

207

208

206 TAXILE DOAT Bottle in the shape of a marrow with pâte-sur-pâte decoration made in Sèvres in 1904.

207 ERNEST BUSSIERE Fruit-shaped vase made in Lunéville. (Collection Félix Marcilhac, Paris)

208 ETIENNE MOREAU-NELATON Vase, 1905.

209 ANDRE METHEY Pitcher. (Collection Félix Marcilhac, Paris)

210 AUGUSTE DELAHERCHE Ceramic vase.

206

209

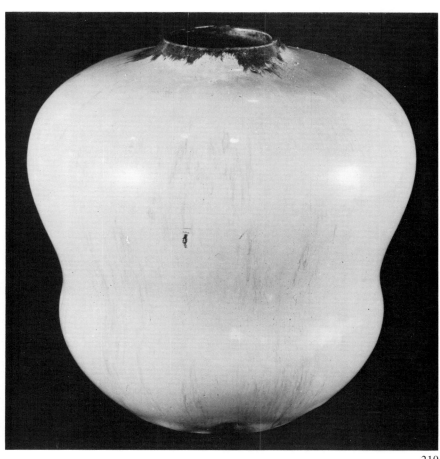

210

211

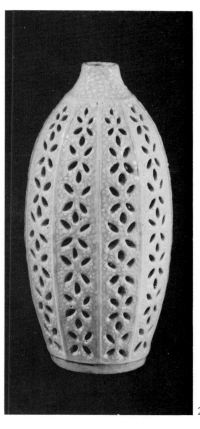

212

211 AUGUSTE DELAHERCHE   Ceramics. (Galerie du Luxembourg, Paris)

212 ANDRE METHEY   Ceramic vase. (Collection Knut Günther)

213

214

2

216

217

218

213 ERNEST CHAPLET Porcelain platter in blue and 'sang-de-boeuf'.

214 GEORGES DE FEURE *Solitaire* service in painted porcelain. (Collection Félix Marcilhac, Paris)

215 CLEMENT MASSIER and LEVY-DHURMER Faience platter made at Golfe-Juan. (Private Collection)

216 FRANÇOIS DECORCHEMONT Stoneware vase, 1903.

217 MAURICE GENSOLI Bottle in whitish-blue porcelain, c.1925. (Collection Félix Marcilhac, Paris)

218 Collection of Art Nouveau ceramics by, clockwise from top left: MAYODON, BIGOT, DELAHERCHE, DECEOUR, DELAHERCHE, DALPAYRAT and JEANNENEY. (Collection Maria de Beyrie)

219

220

219 GEORGES DE FEURE Box, manufactured by Bing Art Nouveau. (Collection Olivier Jaffré)

220 JEAN RINGEL D'ILLZACH Flower pot made according to Ringel d'Illzach's designs by the Chaplet Haviland workshop. (Collection Maria de Beyrie)

221 GEORGES DE FEURE Porcelain vase. (Collection Félix Marcilhac, Paris)

222-223 Sèvres vases. (Mobilier National, Paris)

221

222

223

224

224 WILLIAM MORRIS Embroidered crewel-work hanging, designed in 1877.

225

225 **HECTOR GUIMARD** Stained glass rooflight in the hall of the Hotel Mezzara,
1910-1911.

226 DAUM Vases with glass cabochons in the shape of flowers and leaves applied to the surface. (Collection Jean-Claude Brugnot)

227 DAUM Vase with flower design resulting from several applications of glass.

228 DAUM Vase with tree design etched in acid and engraved with a cutting-wheel into a ground of coloured powdered glass.

229

230

229 EMILE GALLE Group of lamps and a clear glass casket. The small blue lamp
on the left is by Argy-Rousseau. (Collection Maria de Beyrie)

230 LOUIS COMFORT TIFFANY Lamp with a leaded glass shade and a bronze
base, c.1900.

231 **RAOUL LARCHE** *Loïe Fuller*, a gilt-bronze statue with concealed lighting.

232 PIERRE FIX-MASSEAU *Le Secret*, gilt-bronze statue. (Collection Victor
Arwas, London)

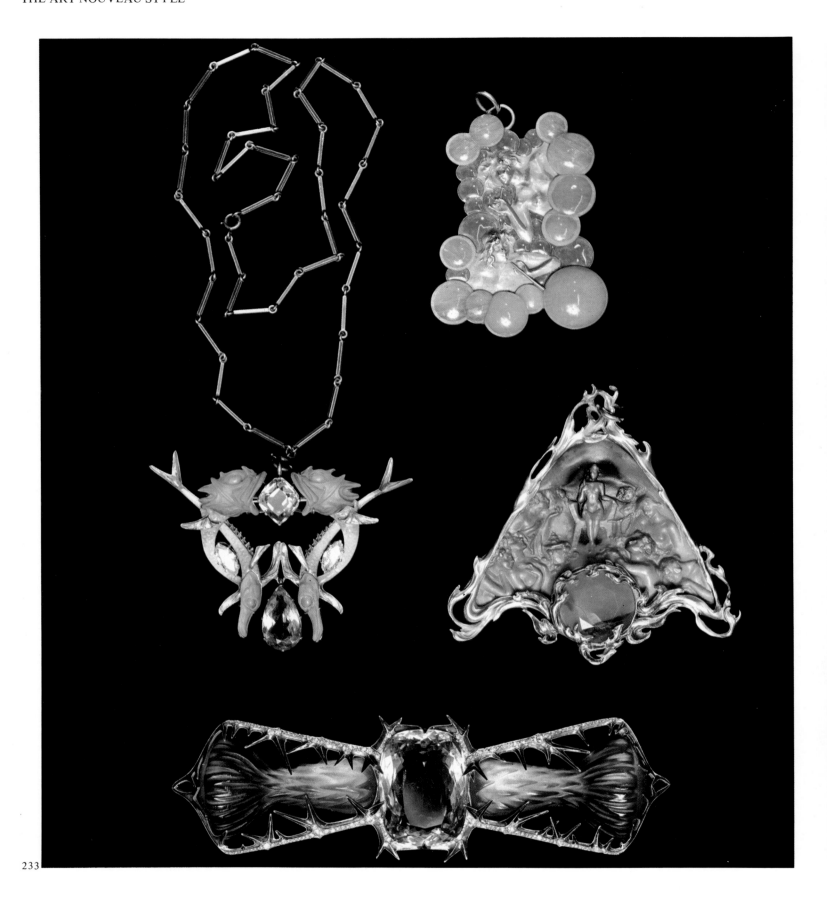

233

233 RENE LALIQUE *(top left) Les Dauphins,* a pendant mounted on gold with pâte-de-verre, translucent and opaque enamel, aquamarine and brilliants; *(top right) Jeunes femmes aux bulles de savon,* consisting of opals on enamelled and engraved gold; *(centre right) Lesbos,* made of coloured horn and opal; *(bottom)* a shoulder brooch based on the theme of the thistle and made of aquamarine surrounded by enamel and brilliants and cut and enamelled crystals. (Private Collection)

GLASS

The art of glassmaking had attained, by the middle of the nineteenth century, a high degree of technical perfection as a result of the widespread adaptation of mechanical means of production. Regularity of form, rigorous faceting by means of cutting and moulding and standardised decoration had replaced the frequently successful effects of chance, and the wealth of invention, characteristic of the works of the glass craftsmen of previous centuries. It would however, be unjust to exaggerate the extent of the absence of good taste amongst these 'industrial craftsmen'. Any lack of artistic sensibility on their part was more than compensated for by their ingenuity and flair for experimentation.

The first signs of a renewal were apparent at the International Exhibition of 1878. Alongside the technical feats accomplished by the bold crystal-glassmakers of Baccarat and Saint-Louis, the refinements of the glass craftsmen of Murano and Bohemia and the creations of Bavaria, Belgium and England, were two French exponents, Joseph Brocard and Emile Gallé who attracted the attention of the public and critics alike by the new tone of their exhibits. The changes could not yet been termed revolutionary, but consisted rather of an initial exploration of new options destined to make an important contribution.

Joseph Brocard already enjoyed considerable renown. He was a dedicated student of Islamic glassware and had rediscovered the secret Oriental process for the decoration of white or tinted glass with enamels. This required painterly skills, consisting of the decoration of each piece with delicate applications of hard, opaque enamels, which might be plain, or coloured in red, white, turquoise, green, blue or gold. He also applied himself to the restoration of mosque lamps and Arabic bowls, and subsequently executed copies and pastiches of his own invention in which elements of Oriental art were combined with themes derived from the Renaissance. Influenced by his young disciples and in particular Emile Gallé, his technique and decorative styles became more widely based. Brocard began to work in glass that was shot through with colour, translucent enamels (dominated by two shades of green), and freely interpreted floral motifs, based on orchids, honesty and mistletoe, with the occasional addition of engraved inscriptions.

In this movement of renewal, Gallé very quickly established himself as an incontestable master. Although a poet, writer, botanist, ceramist and cabinet-maker, it was in glass that he discovered the ideal means of expression for his effervescent personality. Each one of his works is a dialogue between matter and thought, an object impregnated with the soul of its creator. Technique and decoration are no more than a means of expression, the reflection of a philosophic and aesthetic universe of compelling complexity. Dreams are combined with science, mysticism, the love of nature and the region of Lorraine where he was born. The son of a Nancy glassmaker, Gallé attended the Nancy lycée where his brilliant literary studies determined his tastes. After a stay at Weimar, studying Art History, mineralogy and design, Gallé trained for a year (1866-1867) at the glassworks of Meisenthal, in the valley of the Sarre, at that time part of France. On his return, Gallé assumed responsibility for the workshop, founded by his father, for the decoration of earthenware and glass. From the time of the 1867 Exhibition in Paris, Gallé's artistic qualities and knowledge of botany began to be widely remarked upon. He volunteered in 1870 after Sedan, and was deeply affected by the sense of intellectual and social collapse that was occasioned by defeat. The following year, Gallé discovered some newly arrived examples of Far-Eastern art in London and at once became an enthusiast of this art, based on graphic expression, observation of nature, a sense of rite and symbol and respect for craftsmanship.

Initially Gallé hardly deviated at all from the traditional approach of his father's workshop. He retained the dazzlingly limpid, white crystal which had dominated all other pieces and enriched it with the flowers of Lorraine, beautifully designed and engraved with a bow-drill. He then applied himself to the reworking of form, finding inspiration in shells and the corollas of the arum, convolvulus and narcissus. In 1874, Gallé established his own glassmaking concern in Nancy, precipitating the industrial expansion that was to turn the town into an important centre of the applied arts. At the International Exhibition of 1878, Gallé triumphed with a service, intended for everyday use, in a glass known as 'clair de lune,' transparent but coloured with a small quantity of cobalt oxide 'of a rather agreeable sapphire tone', as he himself wrote. This glass was reproduced in England, where it was known as 'moonlight glass' and in Germany where it was called 'mondschein'. During this first period, Gallé also took inspiration from the Oriental methods made fashionable by Brocard: hard Arabic enamels, enamels in relief, 'Japanese style', vitrified at a low temperature and applied on to white or tinted glass. Avoiding the pitfalls of servile imitation, Gallé enlarged his palette with new tones, half tints, grisailles inspired by the stained glass of the Middle Ages, gold and platinum paints and black monochrome designs.

The extent of Gallé's research was revealed when he participated in the Exposition de l'Union Centrale des Arts Décoratifs in 1884. 'Today,' he wrote, 'there is hardly a nuance, no matter how fugitive that does not figure on my palette of enamelled reliefs on glass, from shades of orange and sealing-wax red to violet and purple; these enamels can be over-decorated with soft colours, or leaf metals fastened with a flux.' He also presented some new translucent enamels, combined with opaque enamels, 'which afford the eye a complete satisfaction, whether the piece is examined under a reflected or refracted light'. Gallé combined his enamelled decorations with motifs engraved with a bow-drill. The hard-

234

235

236

237

234 EMILE GALLE *Les Cigales*, an example of carving with the wheel with platinum trapped within the glass. (Collection Jean-Claude Brugnot)

235 EMILE GALLE *Les Libellules*. (Collection Jean-Claude Brugnot)

236 EMILE GALLE Glass vase. (Musée de l'Ecole de Nancy)

237 EMILE GALLE Greyish vase overlaid in dark purple deeply cameo-etched, carved and fire-polished with a continuous pattern of marguerites and leaves with silver mounts at neck and foot, c.1900. (Editions Graphiques Gallery, London)

ness of certain glass made with potash prompted him to create a special drill with a vertical cutting-wheel, designed to penetrate deeply into the material. In addition to this method, Gallé also made use of grindstones and diamond needles for shaping and cutting, and, on rarer occasions, acid baths. His engraver's dexterity permitted him to inscribe quotations and lines of poetry on his vases; a foretaste of the 'talking glassware' of later years.

The International Exhibition of 1889 marked a turning point in Gallé's work. Abandoning transparent glass and enamelled decoration, he inaugurated a new direction for glassware; opacity (which he had initially condemned), and the use of glass shot through with colour. 'This year,' he told the selection committee, 'I am presenting you with a large number of new colours which have rarely been used in glassmaking in the past . . . yellows, browns and greens made iridescent by silver and sulphur, peacock blue produced with copper and iron, and browns from sulphur and cachou.' In addition to the oxides already widely employed, Gallé made use of two rare and costly substances, iridium and thallium (used in the fabrication of the 'agate-rose' urns produced by Falize père and presented to Tsar Nicolas 11 by the town of Paris on October 6 1896).

The use of coloured glass grew more complicated with glasses of various tone being incorporated into the mass, in imitation of hard stones and gems. A streak of pale yellow, derived from sulphur, in amber coloured glass takes on the appearance of a sea-plant. Gallé created these marbled, mottled and clouded effects by a variety of procedures, creating the desired effects by control of heat, by reduction in a closed furnace, or by oxidation with the furnace partly open to allow the flow of oxygen. Imperfections in the quartz, such as cracks, were artifically produced by throwing cold water onto the piece while still being worked under heat by the craftsman. Gallé also introduced 'coloured and reflecting air bubbles', sea-plant designs, butterflies, birds and groups of mossy trees. He incorporated asbestos fibre and flakes of mica into his raw material and introduced leaf metal and other decorations between the layers of glass. His imitations of amber reproduced its natural colour with deceptive accuracy. The lower parts of his pieces, often of hyalite black were deepened with cloudy greens. Some were formed from ordinary glass, others from superimposed, intermingled layers of white, opal and coloured glass, more or less opaque.

Gallé had a liking for 'materials created from an amalgam of superimposed layers, areas of density, motifs, variations in thickness, that are unknown to the glassmaker until he takes up his craft'. He worked his motifs into the surface of the glass, of double or triple thickness, to form tiered reliefs of irregular depth. Though he firmly believed that nothing could replace the hand of the craftsman, he did not ignore the usefulness of acid to obtain certain effects, and sometimes made use of 'its ferocious bite to eat out ornamentations of an archaic style'. A different usage of acid produced effects reminiscent of watercolours. This involved engraving with a pointed instrument onto a protective varnish, the decoration then being deepened with acid, creating effects resembling 'the delicacy of lace'. Treated with a grisaille patina, this form of decoration served as a background against which certain motifs might be emphasised. The 'émaux-bijoux' (translucent jewelled effects created with enamel) stress the delicacy of a detail, animating the eye of a dragonfly with a steely reflected light, or recreating the diaphanous texture of a wing.

The technique of champlevé enamel is comparable to that used to produce incrustations of rock in crystal in the sixteenth century. Cavities are hollowed into the glass, then gilded in the furnace before being filled with several applications of a translucent enamel until level with the surface. It would be impossible to enumerate all the techniques and tricks of which Gallé made use. His exceptional virtuosity served to enforce the engaging ideas and sensitive intelligence of the creative artist. He liked to engrave on his vases – the famous 'verreries parlantes' (talking glassware) – quotations or short poems of his favourite authors such as Victor Hugo, Baudelaire, Rimbaud, Verlaine, Maeterlinck, Mallarmé, Sully-Prudhomme and Marceline Desbordes-Valmore. These are not pedantic allusions, but 'resonances' that illuminate the work, the soul, the thought and the symbolism of Gallé.

This was Matter ruled by Art and Gallé had discovered his direction. In his factory, surrounded by a garden of magnificent flowers, a workshop of composition and design was specially set up for his glass production. Wooden forms were specially shaped to provide blowing instruments, and watercolours and sketches were executed for the enamellers, engravers and painters. The factory garden and Gallé's own

238

238 EMILE GALLE Engraved crystal vase on a silver base by Froment-Meurice, c.1880. (Private Collection)

natural history collection put living nature at the workshop's disposal. The following inscription was sculpted on the door: 'My roots are deep in the woods.' The flower was the object of a cherished cult, 'the symbol of reconciliation with moral beauty, with divinity . . . One word governs all nature, from sign to sign, symbol to symbol, reflection to reflection – and that word is God.' From 1890 onwards, Gallé's decorations forsook all human figuration, the famous vase, *Orphée*, executed in 1889 with the assistance of Victor Prouvé, being the final occasion of its manifestation.

Henceforth fruits, flowers, fauna and aquatic flora were to be the only themes of inspiration. 'The shimmering enigma of waterlilies and pools, the disordered forms of seaweed, the dreams of irises, the glaucous trembling life of shells and fish, all palpitate in his work,' wrote Jean Lorrain.

Forms became freer and inspired in the main by fruits and flowers, the handles of vases were formed by the windings of sinuous branches, coiled into projecting naturalistic volutes. At the Salon des Champs-Elysées in 1892, Gallé presented a range of new tones, as subtle as fluctuations in the weather: 'celestial blue', 'perturbed blue', 'snowy layers of amethyst crystal'. It was also the era of 'glass marquetry', produced by the incorporation, under heat and pressure, of strips of coloured glass into a soft vitreous matter. The result is 'like a complete symphony made up of the many structures that can be formed from vitreous matter'. This marquetry is not to be confused with the soldering of cabochons onto the surface, creating unexpected rhythms. Gallé disregarded the elementary laws of equilibrium and geometry. His work conformed to no plan, no governing imperative; it sprang forth with joyful liveliness, to the detriment of all formulas. It reflected the whole man, his political convictions, his patriotic and social aspirations: at the time of the Dreyfus affair, he produced *dreyfusard* vases and similarly the *Pasteur* bowl commissioned by the Ecole Normale Supérieure, was a meditation on modern science.

Gallé's contribution to the 1900 Exhibition was a fresh and original display of pyrotechnics that won him considerable acclaim. Even his most vehement detractors were silenced by the display of such invention, science and virtuosity. No one before him had succeeded in glorifying glass, in harnessing its expressive potential, to such an extent that it rivalled the most precious of objects and materials. His work was equal to the unique objects, the 'vitrified poems' produced by the greatest gold and silversmiths of the time: Cardeilhac, Falize père, Froment-Meurice, Joseph Joindry and Francis Peureux.

Gallé continued to exercise his flair for invention until his premature death in 1904. In his final works he perfected new patinas which were produced, according to Jules Henrivaux, 'by the treatment of the surface of the glass by controlled exposure to heat or to a special atmosphere, or by dusting with organic or mineral powders'. In this manner he reproduced the effects of fog, rain and flakes of snow and imitated brocaded materials and leather. But these works, inspite of their originality, cannot compete with those of Gallé's greatest period of creativity, between 1880 and 1890.

Emile Gallé, the creator of genius, was also an astute businessman. By 1900 he was employing three hundred people in his workshops, had opened retail shops in a number of towns and organised mass-production. Vases were produced, formed from two layers of glass and engraved with acid that reflected a minimal interpretation of his art. This artistic vulgarisation was justified by Gallé's social ideals, and his desire to see beauty penetrate to all areas of society. 'In my less expensive productions,' he wrote, 'I have avoided the false, the distorted, the fragile . . . I have widened the scope of crystal glass and prepared the way, sometimes to my own detriment, for profitable large-scale factory production. If this has led to the appearance of 'Gallé style' imitations, then I am not displeased.'

After Gallé's death, production continued in a simplified form until 1913. The materials were standardised, and colour arrangements popular with the public, such as manganese violet against an opaque white background, were too often repeated. Though the 'Gallé style' lived on in these pieces, they were obviously far removed from the true spirit of the craftsman, poet and magician of glass.

Almost all Gallé's works were signed by the artist and bear signatures that rival his decorations for baroque fantasy. Several types of signature can be distinguished amongst the many examples: the manuscript signature, complete or simply the initials, enamelled or engraved and sometimes accompanied by the cross of Lorraine, or by a brief quotation which appears mostly on the early works; the signature in relief, vertical or horizontal, which appears on items formed from several layers of superimposed glass, or on glass imitations of precious stones; the moulded signature that appears on the industrially produced items (the presence of a star indicating that the work post-dates Gallé's death); signatures engraved with hydroflouric acid which figure on the mass-produced items and signatures accompanied by the mark of the workshop which distinguish the pieces executed by Gallé's assistants but under his direction.

The 1884 Exposition des Arts Décoratifs saw the triumph of a contemporary of Gallé's, the Parisian, Eugène Rousseau (1827-1891). Well-known as a dealer, in the rue Coquillière, and as a man of taste and initiative (he was responsible for the success of the famous Bracquemond service), he was also interested in glass. Initially, Rousseau commissioned other artists, such as Alphonse Reyen who was an engraver and decorator of glass, to make pieces according to his designs. His first objective was to recreate glass tableware in a style that was inspired by archaeology, yet also wholly original. His models were also influenced by German 'vidrecoms' (large drinking glasses) and by ecclesiastical pieces in gold and silver from the Renaissance and from the Far East. In 1884 Rousseau exhibited a Louis XIV display cabinet ornamented with a grotesque mask of gold, a fish vase of smoked glass thickened with a reddish-brown glass in imitation of sardonyx, vases in mock-agate and cups animated by dim reflections. With the aid of a bow-drill and acid, he inscribed strange motifs, sculpted in cameo of a brick-red or coral colour, onto the ambered surface of the thickened glass. The rich and precious quality of the material was obtained by a series of manipulations under heat. Small cracks were introduced into the glass to create a tracery of brilliant luminosity. Golden flakes sparkle from within the thickness of the glass, and gold leaf, positioned beneath the motifs in relief, emanates a deep luminous glow. Seduced, like all glass craftsmen, by precious gems, Rousseau succeeded in imitating jade, sardonyx, agate and amethyst.

239

240

241

242

239 EMILE GALLE Group of early works with, in the centre, the beautiful flacon decorated with a bat. (Collection Maria de Beyrie)

240 EMILE GALLE *Les Pensées,* glass inlaid vase. (Collection Félix Marcilhac, Paris)

241 EMILE GALLE Glass inlaid vase. (Collection Félix Marcilhac, Paris)

242 DAUM Cameo vase wheel-carved with a floral pattern, hammered ground c.1900. (Editions Graphiques Gallery, London)

'His hands turn everything to gems,' wrote Louis de Fourcaud in the general report of the 1884 Exhibition. 'Glass turns to a rose-hued crimson on contact with gold oxide, borrows from manganese the violet transparence of amethyst, is splashed with blood at the touch of copper oxide or displays traces of a luminous tin-derived yellow light, like a gilded oil, in its glowing fissures.' Rousseau preceded Gallé as a maker of false stones and no doubt incited him to follow the same path. By means of the projection of powdered glass and metallic oxides, Rousseau obtained new effects. Sometimes the metals spread out to produce tree-like forms within the translucent mass.

In 1885, Eugène Rousseau made a partner of one of his disciples, Ernest Léveillé, who after Rousseau's death became his successor. Like his mentor, he was very influenced by Japanese art and he followed the same traditions: the imitation of hard stones, the use of glass that is smoked, frosted, shot-through with colour or clouded red or green and cameo decorations. They are seductive works, but they lack the powerful and controlled sense of invention that characterised Rousseau's pieces.

In Nancy itself, the effervescent creativity of Emile Gallé gave rise, amongst the glass craftsmen, to a salutary emulation. Paul Nicolas, a trained botanist, executed floral decorations and the Muller brothers, who also worked with Gallé until his death, subsequently moved to Lunéville and then to Croismare. Finally there were the Daum brothers, Auguste (1853-1909) and Antonin (1864-1930) installed in their own business and whose important contribution should not be underestimated. Their father, Jean Daum, had come from Alsace and established himself in Nancy in 1871. The items produced in his workshop were for everyday use and possessed no great originality; his tableware for example was of a traditional style, inspired by the creations of the eighteenth century in France. However, his second son Antonin, who became active in the business from 1887, brought with him a new approach. From 1890, when Gallé was in the ascendant, Antonin surrendered to his influence and to the concepts of Art Nouveau. His first vases, decorated with painted flowers copied straight from nature, in particular, cow-parsley, in gold and enamels, were in accordance with the naturalistic style prevalent in Nancy. The flowers and plants were followed by insects, storks and landscapes treated in the same style.

The Daum brothers were skilful organisers and opened up new workshops for the production of 'artistic glassware', which was the most interesting branch of their activities. They no longer executed their own decorations, but surrounded themselves with painters and decorators of talent who furnished them with models in the spirit of Art Nouveau. The originality of these creations lies less in the quality of the decoration than in the diversity of the techniques. Several processes were sometimes used for one single piece but since it would be irksome to study them all, it will be sufficient to confine our attention to those most common to the Daum's production.

The most prevalent were engraved motifs, embellished with gold and touches of enamel, raised in low relief on a frosted background. These items, in transparent or opalescent glass, were plunged into a bath of hydrofluoric acid to give them a frosted appearance. The motifs were protected during this process and afterwards coated with coloured enamels to create a precious effect.

Other pieces were formed from superimposed layers of coloured glass, engraved with acid. The acid was made to bite into the layers of different coloured glass, to form motifs composed of subtle modulations of tone in a variety of tints. These works are free of any enamel embellishments. The coloured motifs, in projecting relief, are composed of particles of tinted glass, and represent what remains after the action of the acid on the layers of glass.

Layered decorations were the result of highly skilled technical performances which took one of several forms. The most complex of these has been described by Antonin Daum. 'A basic form is decorated, engraved or cut through several layers of glass, it is then brought back to the temperature of the fusion of glass, covered with further layers drawn from the furnace and shaped into its final form of cup or vase. The piece is then thoroughly worked with a wheel, penetrating through the reliefs formed on the surface of the vase to reveal the imprisoned motifs inscribed upon the inner walls, linking them to the general decoration, at times scarcely touching the surface of the vase, then plunging into the vaporous mass of the glass. It is an extremely difficult and complicated process, and all credit should rest with the glassblower for those rare occasions when he meets with success.' A simplified version was achieved by inserting enamelled decorations between two layers of glass. Finally, powdered enamels were used to give a speckled appearance to glass, or to impregnate its transparence, creating a tonal impression evocative of precious stones. Compositions of this type were frequently used for lamps, chandeliers and ceiling lights.

Vitrification was another procedure, by which powdered enamels were disposed on the surface of the glass, then vitrified in the furnace. The piece takes on an iridescent appearance with multiple splashes of colour that are sometimes elaborated with a cutting wheel into flower or leaf forms.

A further process was the application of pieces of glass soldered under heat onto the surface in order to form motifs.

Incrustations were part of a technique similar to Emile Gallé's production of glass marquetry. Small slabs of glass of a variety of colours were thrust into the surface of the vase, while still soft, to various depths. The contours of the motifs were then picked out by engraving.

All of the pieces produced by the Daum workshops after 1890 bore signatures. Between 1890 and 1914 there were essentially three types: manuscript signatures painted in gold (from 1890 to 1896); heavily engraved signatures, sometimes picked out in gold and signatures in relief, usually to be found on mediocre items composed of two or more layers of glass. As a rule, the Daum signature was accompanied by the name of the town of Nancy, and by the cross of Lorraine.

The greater part of the output of Amalric Walter (1859-1942) was carried out in the Daum workshops between 1906 and 1914, when he established his own business. He seems however to have enjoyed considerable independence within the Daum organisation at Nancy. His principal achievement was the perfection of the pâte-de-verre technique, in which the Daum brothers were also interested. In addition to a large number of small cups, on the sides of which would be placed a small animal (frog, lizard etc.), he executed numerous figurines, of personages or animals, reproductions of works both classical (Greek statuettes, the Venus de Milo) and modern (such as the statuette of the dancer Loïe Fuller, based on a design by Victor Prouvé). The designer Henry Bergé, who worked with the Daums, also provided Walter with a number of models.

Pâte-de-Verre

It is essential to differentiate between glass and pâte-de-verre, since the composition of these two materials differs radically. Glass is formed from well-known ingredients, while pâte-de-verre is created by filling a mould with powdered glass or crystal, which is then placed in the furnace. Pâte-de-verre is never transparent; its surface is matt and grainy, or frosted, in appearance. It has often been confused with other types of glass, produced by more elaborate procedures of the type employed by Gallé, though he never used this method.

Painter, sculptor and ceramist, Henri Cros (1840-1907) also earned the nickname, 'l'homme de la pâte-de-verre'. It was he alone who rediscovered, in about 1884, the secret of this material, which had been known to the Egyptians and probably the Greeks, if Pliny the Younger is to be believed. He was the brother of the surrealist poet Charles Cros, but his interests were always oriented towards the plastic arts. He produced a complete series of sculpture-paintings in coloured wax, based on a combination of mediaeval and antique themes. Cros was passionately interested in classical art and made a study of its techniques, leading to the publication of a work, written in conjunction with Charles Henry, entitled *L'Encaustique et les autres procédés de peinture chez les Anciens*. When he rediscovered pâte-de-verre, Cros saw the plasticity of this material as providing a means of recreating polychrome sculpture. The Sèvres manufacturers took an interest in his research and, in 1892, put a workshop at his disposal. He produced not only some statuettes, which possessed a strange charm, but also immense bas-reliefs entitled *L'Histoire de l'Eau* (1894), *L'Histoire du Feu* (which received the gold medal at the 1900 Exhibition) and the *Apothéose de Victor Hugo* (1905). He never revealed the full truth about his methods and one can only marvel at the effects he obtained from the contrast between the rugged material and his subtle colouring and the way in which he concealed visual traces of the assembling of his bas-reliefs. These were classical compositions of great distinction, expressionistic by virtue of their powerfulness of gesture, and of a philosophical conception that married antique purity with the symbolism of Art Nouveau. His perfectly mastered technique did not always succeed in masking the limitations of his material in terms of sculptural expression.

Cros' example encouraged others, including his pupil Georges Despret (1862-1952) who was not only a glass craftsman, but a painter and ceramist also. (Officially he was a maker of mirrors, and a director of the Jeumont factories). Like his teacher, Despret worked in pâte-de-verre endeavouring to rediscover the ancient techniques, the sumptuous aspect of the Murrhine vases evoked by Pliny and Cicero. Most of his production consisted of statuettes and other ornaments, made from monochrome pastes in dull tones which were decorative pieces rather than works of art.

Albert Dammouse also worked with Henri Cros and was himself a sculptor, painter and in particular a ceramist already well-known when he exhibited some delicate pieces at the Salon in 1898; such as small vases, bowls, cups and goblets made from a beautifully refined substance of blue or mauve tone. This material, similar to pâte-de-verre was sometimes called for no particular reason, pâte-d'émail. It nevertheless allowed Dammouse to be placed amongst the innovators in glasswork materials. He continued to produce, until the end of his life, objects possessing a discreet gracefulness, from whose slender forms emerged, as in a dream, seaweed and tiny flowers tinted with matt enamels.

A painter and later a ceramist, François Décorchemont (1880-1971) was born at Conches, where he lived and worked until his death, apart from some brief interludes in Paris. It was after 1900 that he became interested in glass, relying on a very personal rule-of-thumb technique. He used the usual components of glass (sand and a melting agent) mixed with a binding jelly made from quince pips. This pâte-d'émail (an ambiguous term, as has already been noted) was then pressed in a mould. The artist later removed it and reworked it 'in the raw', before replacing it in a mould for heating. In 1907 or 1908, influenced by the work of Dammouse, Décorchemont began to work in pâte-de-verre or more exactly pâte-de-cristal. He purchased his crystal from the manufacturers of Saint-Denis, crushed it in a crucible with different oxides to produce the desired tint, then placed it all in a kiln. After being removed from the kiln the block of crystal was always crushed by hand and never pounded mechanically. The resultant powder was used as the basic material for all of Décorchemont's works; vases, cups, bas-reliefs and stained glass, produced by means of a series of complex empirical operations that would be difficult to describe here. In terms of both their form and decoration, these works share a common sculptural quality, powerful rhythms and a richness and subtlety of colour.

Gabriel Argy-Rousseau (1885-1953) was an accomplished craftsman in glass who also used pâte-de-verre. He introduced a technique for colouring the surface of his material whereby his pieces, already baked were coated with a powdery oxide, then reheated to a lower temperature. In addition to his vases, lamps and cups, he joined with Bouvaine to experiment with sculpture.

Though a goldsmith by profession, René Lalique (1860-1945) was primarily the inventor of a new art jewellery. He was deeply influenced by the symbolism of the times and did not recoil from adapting the most audacious techniques and means of expression. Lalique never hesitated when forming his gems into arrangements of sumptuous enchantment before adding elements of moulded glass or engraved crystal. At the 1901 Salon, Lalique's window was framed by two large crystal snakes, to the astonishment of the visitors. But it was only in 1907 that he produced his first perfume bottles, introducing his art into a domaine that had previously been the reserve of industry. He endeavoured from the beginning to retain the limpid, transparent quality of his material and then went on to perfect several types of glass from which not only bottles, but tableware, small figurines, animals and personages could be produced. Unlike Gallé, Lalique did not aim to express his philosophy through his work. He accepted the modern conditions of work and mechanical procedures in particular for moulding, which were better suited to the exigencies of mass-production. He rarely made use of the

243

244

245

243 DAUM Crystal vase.

244-245 DAUM Vases with a flower motif showing the artists' skill and ingenuity with pâte-de-verre. (Collection Alain Lesieutre, Paris)

246 ALBERT DAMMOUSE Vase. (Collection Félix Marcilhac, Paris)

247 ERNEST LEVEILLE Vase. (Collection Félix Marcilhac, Paris)

248 MULLER Pâte-de-verre vase. (Collection Andrée Vyncke)

246

247

249 RENE LALIQUE Engraved silver and opaque blown glass chalice. (Collection Félix Marcilhac, Paris)

250 HENRI CROS Pâte-de-verre polychrome plaque moulded with an amazon on horseback, c.1895. (Collection Félix Marcilhac, Paris)

251 GEORGES DE FEURE Two moulded glass vases in streaked purple glass and pitcher with acid-finished surface, c.1910. (Private Collection, London)

252 FRANÇOIS DECORCHEMONT Mask and floating fish in pâte-de-cristal. (Collection Andrée Vyncke)

253 White crystal flacons engraved on the theme of Neptune and Amphitrite with silver mounts and shell stoppers, made in Hainaut, France.

248

249

25

251

252

253

bow-drill or applications of enamel to give his work finish. The major part of his work was produced in the 20s and belongs in the main to the period known as Art Deco.

Louis-Comfort Tiffany (1848-1933) was to the United States what Gallé was to France: the symbol of Art Nouveau. He opened new paths to American art at a time when it was stagnating in a traditional Early American style. From a family of goldsmiths and jewellery-makers, he was himself a goldsmith, painter and above all, glass craftsman. He studied in Paris up to 1878 and executed his first experimental works with Heidt of Brooklyn. He was also an industrial designer of considerable scope. In 1879 Tiffany founded the Tiffany Glass and Decorating Company which, besides producing objects in glass, undertook the decoration of vast private and official interiors, including the White House. In 1892 Tiffany set up a new workshop to specialise in glassblowing, according to his specifications. There the glass was treated with chemicals and vaporised metals in fusion, to produce precious iridescent effects similar to those characteristic of ancient excavated glass. Exhibited for the first time in Chicago in 1893, this glass

254 LOUIS COMFORT TIFFANY Vase. (Collection Alain Lesieutre, Paris)

enjoyed an immense success. It was generally known as Favrile Glass, derived from the ancient English word 'fabrile' meaning 'made by hand'. This term was invented by Tiffany himself, who had it officially registered in 1894. It included not only iridescent glass, but different categories of glass and other materials (ceramics, metals), worked under the direct control of the creator. For the customer and the future collector it was an unquestionable guarantee.

The vases executed by Tiffany were sometimes inspired by Persian models and sometimes by plant forms, blooming into corollas and calyxes and thrusting forth their pliant stems. These supple free forms of naturalistic inspiration were easily developed to the point of abstraction. At other times the form was of small importance, the richness and novelty of the piece residing in the material itself. Filaments, nervures and colour traces incorporated into the paste suggest the delicacy of a petal, the velvety texture of a fruit. Tiffany also created vases that were opaque and matt, surprisingly soft to the touch and enriched with cabochons and flows of different coloured glass. He never surrendered to the temptation to imitate gems or other precious substances. His determination to invent his own materials was reaffirmed in each one of his works.

Tiffany supervised the production of thousands of objects, which were distributed throughout the world. Samuel Bing, his agent in Paris, made an important contribution to this success and like Gallé, influenced many other artists, in particular the glassmakers of Bohemia. But his sense of imagination and the particular way in which he organised his effects of marbling and flow were inimitable.

Tiffany's success coincided with the arrival, initially in the United States, of electric lighting so it is only natural that he should have been one of the first creators of incandescent lamps. Skilled with both metals and glass, Tiffany worked in bronze and glass together to form lamp-shades made up of mosaics, mounting his fragments of coloured glass in a network of bronze threads, as in the manner of cloisonné enamels. His decorative themes were often of floral inspiration (poppies, hydrangeas, jonquils, wistaria etc.) and occasionally geometric (arachnoid ornamentations, mottled like the wing of a dragonfly).

Tiffany was also the author of numerous items of stained glass, executed from his own sketches or those made for him by several artists (particularly Brangwyn) at the request of Samuel Bing. He made use of a variety of techniques attaching little importance to the subject matter, but forming strange harmonies of colour and material. The superimposing of layers of glass, the creation of streaks of colour and chance effects and the incorporation of natural elements (pebbles and gems that have been polished, ground or set) filter the light in a curious fashion 'as if through a cloud-filled sky'. At the 1900 Exhibition he presented stained glass that had been poured and moulded to an irregular thickness in imitation of ancient stained glass. All painted or enamelled embellishments were denounced.

After winning the Grand Prix at the Turin Exhibition of 1902, Tiffany devoted himself henceforth to jewellery. In 1918, his home at Oyster Bay, Long Island, became a centre for artists whom he supported financially and whose works he helped to execute.

255 LOUIS COMFORT TIFFANY Moorish lamp with glass shade and metal
mounts and pottery base by Clément Massier. A rare example of Tiffany's collaboration
with European artists, c.1895-1910.

256 LOUIS COMFORT TIFFANY Tel El Amarna vase with matt lustred surface
in rich blue.

57

258

259

257-259 LOUIS COMFORT TIFFANY Collection of lustred, iridescent and millefiore vases with pulled thread decoration. (Collection Alain Lesieutre, Paris)

260

261

262

260 RENE LALIQUE   Vase with seascape design in brownish-red giving the appearance of hard stone.

261 RENE LALIQUE   Vase with particles of gold leaf trapped within the layers of glass and based on a line by Musset: *Je récolte en secret des fleurs mystérieuses.*

262 RENE LALIQUE   Another poem interpreted in glass: *Nymphe de l'eau vive, La Carpe naive, Du jeu des amours, se prendra toujours.* The two vases are mounted on carved wooden pedestals. (Private Collection)

CLOCKS

The clock not only marks time: it fixes it. Its hands turn within a self-contained environment of metal or wood, conceived by the artisan — goldsmith or sculptor — in accordance with the spirit of his age. The elegant themes of Louis XV and Louis XVI and the mythological evocations of the early nineteenth century were superseded in 1900 by the cult for plantlife and the female form. An ordered sense of line, as prescribed by classical authority was usurped almost completely by curvilinear floral abundancy and animated scenes.

263 JACQUES GRUBER Ceramic clock with floral motif. (Collection Jeanne Fillion)

264 Gilt -bronze clock. (Collection Jeanne Fillion)

265 Small clock incorporated within the bust of a young woman. (Private Collection)

266 WILLIAM HUTTON Solid silver and enamelled mother-of-pearl clock. (Collection Alain Lesieutre, Paris)

267 HECTOR GUIMARD Gilt-bronze clock. (Collection Félix Marcilhac, Paris)

268 EUGENE GRASSET Clock face set in raised stoneware. (Galerie du Luxembourg, Paris)

269 LOUIS MAJORELLE Carved and inlaid clock case. (Collection Félix Marcilhac, Paris)

270 GEORGES DE FEURE Clock.

263

264

265

266

267

268

269

270

271 NOVAK   Small mantlepiece clock. (Collection Manoukian, Paris)

272 RENOIR   Clock. (Boston Museum)

273 BONNEFOND   Silvered metal clock. (Private Collection)

274 ESTERAZ   Clock. (Ferpoël Castle, Hungary)

272

73

274

MIRRORS

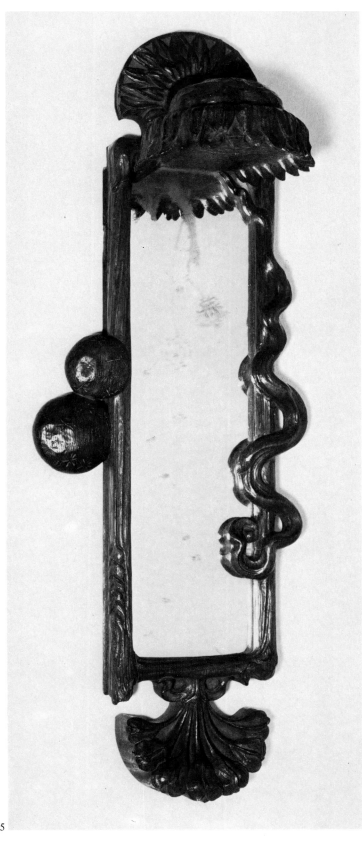

27●

27●

275 Engraved mirror in a wooden frame. (Musée de l'Ecole de Nancy)

276 MATTEI Moulded and painted metal mirror. (Collection Duret Robert)

277 Carved wooden frame for a mirror. (Collection Manoukian, Paris)

278 Natural wood frame made by a student of William Morris. (Collection Alain Lesieutre, Paris)

279 C. BONNEFOND Gilt-wood mirror with a stand at the back to enable it to rest upright on a dressing-table. (Collection M. and Mme B.)

280 Embossed copper mirror. (Private Collection)

275

278

279

280

OBJETS D'ART AND THE FEMALE FORM

The craftsmen, because they rejected all the tired disciplines of the nineteenth century, claimed to have reinvented everything and indeed, those who created objects that were completely free of the past were innumerable. Most of them wanted to invest their work with meaning and took to symbolism with commitment and enthusiasm. Thus the vases, statuettes and ash-trays that we see today, require us to see beyond the subject and discern the message. Gallé, even when drawing a flower with the utmost precision did so with the intention of telling us something. And so an orchid, placed against a background of Japanese inspiration, became a symbol of fertility. Dreams were also an important source of creative inspiration. It was Gallé again who, remembering just how much a single informal motif can evoke for each one of us, wrote: 'Sometimes I amuse myself by creating accidents that become objects, zestful little games, baroque problems based on variegated materials that question the imagination. In this way the gaze of the invalid transforms a crumpled sheet of fancy paper into a thousand strange shapes and the setting sun that appears to a child as an immense pastoral, evokes jagged capes and beaches in the eye of the sailor.'

281 Liqueur cabinet pulled by a still in the shape of a train, underneath which is the small stove. (Private Collection)

282

282 Objets d'art typical of the Art Nouveau period on a table by Majorelle. (Collection Manoukian, Paris)

Carabin was not the only one to make of the female body an essential element of the new style, for while he was integrating it into his furniture, other artists were making it the theme of their bronzes and the principal subject of their clocks, vases, lamps and ash-trays. One might find this surprising at a time when fashion and modesty compelled women to don long, high-collared dresses. It may have been a consequence of the return to nature or simply the fact that these highly sculpted objects were executed by artists who were accustomed in their workshops to study the nude.

283-285 Three small bronzes based on the female form.

283

284

285

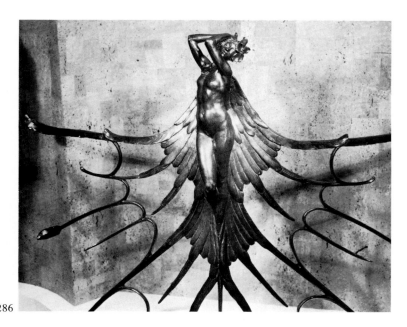

286

286 RENE LALIQUE *Femme au cygne* in wrought-iron, part of a set of four similar pieces displayed at the Paris 1900 Exhibition. (Private Collection)

287 PHILIPPE WOLFERS *La Femme au paon.* Behind the coloured cabochons, small lights were inserted in the tail of the peacock.

288 Richly decorated casket, the central motif of which is a naked female figure by Victor Prouvé. (Musée de l'Ecole de Nancy)

289 LAMARRE *La Femme libellule,* a ceramic and gilt-bronze vase mounted with bronze lily-pads, flowers and woman with plique-à-jour enamel wings, 1898. (Collection Manoukian, Paris)

290 CHARLES KORSCHANN Gilt metal ash-tray. (Private Collection)

291 Pewter vase.

292 *L'Annonciation,* a bronze and ivory statue three feet high. (Collection Jean-Claude Brugnot)

287

288

289

290

291

292

293

29

295

293 Large pewter vase crowned by a mermaid. (Private Collection)

294 RENE LALIQUE   Silver, ivory and enamel vase, with sculpted figures attributed to Rodin. (Private Collection)

295 Pewter vide-poche. (Private Collection)

296

297

296 WURTTEMBERGISCHE METALLWARENFABRIK (W.M.F.) Electro-
plated metal visiting card tray. (Maclowe Gallery)

297 Gilt-bronze inkwell with designs by Arnoux. (Collection Christolfe)

298

299

METALWORK

300

301

302

298 BAPST and FALIZE Silver tea-service highlighted in gold and made in 1889.

299 Bread basket with designs by Arnoux. (Collection Christofle)

300 EDWARD COLONNA White metal teapot.

301 E. BOURGOUIN Chalice from the Christofle atelier. (Musée des Arts Décoratifs, Paris)

302 HECTOR GUIMARD Gilt-bronze platter. (Musée des Arts Décoratifs, Paris)

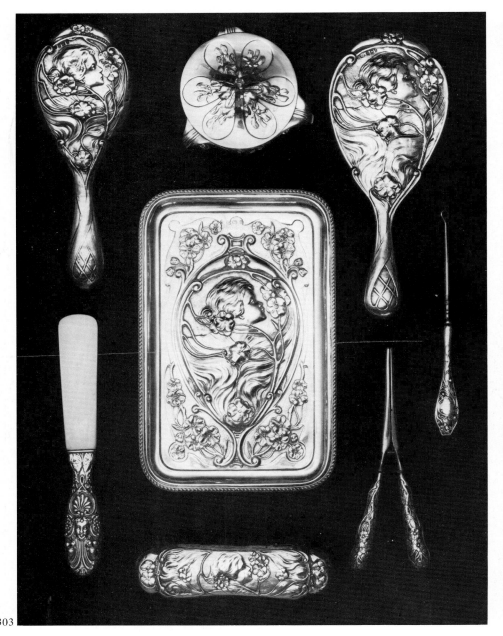

303

304

305

303 Silver dressing-table set made in England which once belonged to Sarah Bernhardt.

304 C. BONNEFOND Candlestick.

305 EMILE GALLE Silver candlesticks.

144

306 CHARLES JONCHERY *Agonie de Lis*, patinated metal candlestick. (Private Collection)

307 White metal boxes.

308 White metal platter.

309 Pewter dish. (Private Collection)

310

311

312

310 Gilt-bronze card holder.

311 H. SIBEUD Silvered bronze vase. (Private Collection)

312 H. SORENSEN *La Nuit*, a gilt-bronze statuette. (Collection Andrée Vyncke)

313 SALESIO Bronze lamp. The electric bulbs, when inserted form an integral part of the flowers. (Collection Andrée Vyncke)

314

315

316

317

314 MULLER Two card holders, one of silvered bronze and the other of gilt-bronze.

315 EUGENE FEUILLATRE Enamel and gold cup on which is balanced a gilt-bronze woman.

316 Gilt-bronze female figure holding a lamp in her veil. (Private Collection)

317 *Salomé*, a gilt-bronze statuette on a marble base. (Collection Andrée Vyncke)

318

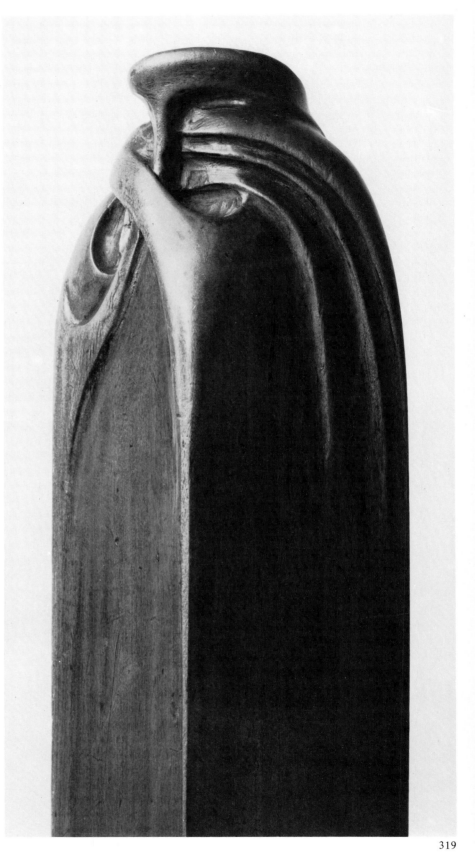

319

320

318 HECTOR GUIMARD Bronze vase. (Collection Alain Blondel and Yves Plantin)

319 HECTOR GUIMARD Bronze vase. (Galerie du Luxembourg, Paris).

320 RAOUL LARCHE Bronze and wrought-iron bowl. (Collection Manoukian, Paris)

JEWELLERY

It was in the domaine of jewellery that the aspirations and dreams of the creators of Art Nouveau were expressed with the most intensity. Painters, architects, sculptors and decorators joined forces with gold and silversmiths to produce the most extravagant and poetic regalia, forms that often retained the rigorous clarity of a working drawing. Faithful to the principle of unity in art, they aimed to invest this supposedly minor art with a sense of style of magnificent and prestigious proportions.

But what did jewellery represent up to the end of the Second Empire? It was an object of adornment, certainly, but also an investment and an unmistakable sign of wealth and power. In Paris this tradition was represented by certain goldsmiths and jewellery-makers of renown: Froment-Meurice, Cardeilhac, Sandoz, Aucoc, Bapst and Falize. Sweeping aside these concepts, Art Nouveau jewellery became the symbol of an aesthetic and moral stance. It was a synthesis of all forms of artistic and literary creation, imposing a new attitude and suggesting a way of life.

This sudden upheaval was to some extent analogous to that which brought about the Renaissance. In each one finds the same exaltation of matter, the same taste for the baroque, for hallucinations and a certain mannerism. Rare gems are used alongside horn, ivory and amber; but traditional techniques are retained and frenzied imagination does not compromise respect for craftsmanship. This orientation was asserted in the course of a succession of major exhibitions in Paris. Elements of fantasy appeared after 1889, but did not yet go beyond the imitation of nature. Newcomers, including Boucheron, Cartier, Templier, Massin, Vever, Fouquet and, above all, Lalique committed themselves in 1894 to the new way. The following year, Lalique triumphed at the Salon du Champ de Mars, followed by Fouquet, Feuillâtre, Vever and Gaillard. 1900 marked the apotheosis of ever more daring creations, conceived, wrote a critic, as if 'to decorate the

head of a Gorgon, rather than to adorn the warm perfumed bosom of a pretty Parisienne.' Across surfaces of white watered silk, Lalique arranged 'strange monsters, hydras or dragons, nightmarish visions, fantastic tormented beings, vomiting flames or dribbling greenish enamels'. Apart from these extravagances, the decorative repertoire was enriched with new elements borrowed from fauna and flora. The mistletoe, waterlily, orchid, poppy, iris, thistle and convolvulus vied with the snake, jelly-fish, octopus, bat and owl for pride of place. Boutet de Monvel, painter and creator of jewellery, aspired to adorn women with 'the most vile beasts of creation'. More decorative were swans and peacocks depicted in sparkling, delicate stones, and the mottled wings of the dragonfly, composed of iridescent enamelled reflections. Lalique reintroduced the human figure, for the first time since the Renaissance, into his creations, depicting woman as a butterfly or a dragonfly or in the languid form of a sylph.

Jean Lorrain was filled with enthusiasm for these pendants, displaying female nudes 'cut from some stone of mysterious origin, transparent and pink as flesh, and surrounded by flowerings of majestic iris composed of greenish gold foliage and opal blooms'. Opal had not yet acquired its malefic associations and was the most characteristic stone of Art Nouveau. The traditional precious stones tended to be spurned in favour of gems of rare colour, hard stones shot through with twisted veins, baroque pearls and in particular, iridescent enamels of a translucent or opaque quality and a concise literary symbolism was added to the aesthetic dimension. The parallels between these adornments and the poems of Baudelaire, Mallarmé and other 'decadents' are multiple. A piece of jewellery created by Georges de Feure for Bing was inspired by an emblem of Alciati. One can also pick out the influence of Japanese art, a revival of ancient myths like the theme of the girl/flower, illustrated in Parsifal or the perfidious Hérodiade, the woman and the serpent.

321 Blue enamel bracelet with sapphires and brilliants. (Private Collection)

321

322

323

322 GEORGES FOUQUET Dragonfly brooch in green translucent enamel with rubies and a baroque pearl. (Private Collection)

323 GEORGES FOUQUET Translucent enamel and pearl pendant. (Private Collection)

324 GEORGES FOUQUET Gold pendant with opals and green enamel. (Private Collection)

325 RENE LALIQUE Engraved gold cuff-links. (Private Collection)

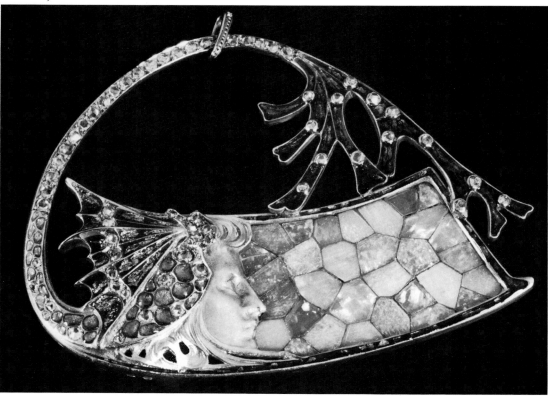

325

324

Who were the women who dared to wear these adornments, sometimes referred to as 'shop-window pieces' or 'theatrical jewellery'? A number of them were, indeed, designed for Sarah Bernhardt, Julia Bartet and Marguerite Moreno. Courtesans in a class with La Belle Otero and Liane de Pougy, took them up with enthusiasm. But the 'grandes dames', as ostentatious under the Third Republic as they had been under the Second Empire, and the Russian princesses, did not shy away from the showrooms of Vever and Fouquet. Only the traditional bourgeoisie, faithful to the principle of financial investment, were wary of Art Nouveau jewellery.

René Lalique began by supplying models to the great jewellers of Paris: Jacta, Aucoc, Cartier, Renn, Gariod and finally Destape, whose workshop he took over in 1896. Lalique was an excellent draughtsman and dedicated worker who had studied sculpture and designed wallpapers and materials before devoting himself to glasswork and jewellery. His complex personality was similar to that of Gallé, possessing the same love of nature, choosing the same plants and animals and tending towards the same interest in symbolism and dreams. These two men were admirably in tune with their time and its modes of expression.

Every occasion on which Lalique sent his work to the Salons constituted an artistic event. Very quickly, his work emerged from amongst that of his peers as 'richer, more disturbing, and, in the words of Shakespeare, of the essence of many things'. Through his choice of themes and materials, Lalique liberated himself from tradition and introduced into his jewellery every form of audacity of which his effervescent imagination could conceive. For Sarah Bernhardt, he executed luxuriously decorated jewellery designed for specific roles. Julia Bartet ordered a diadem 'with winged figures inspired by Isis, lotus flowers and five scenes from the lives of courtesans'. This theatrical lyricism did not stop him from using materials that had been scorned in the past: horn, ivory, coral, rock crystal, agate, cornelian, onyx, enamel and glass. 'None knew better than he how to bring out the baroque charm of a pearl, to display a faulty cabochon or mount a jewel to best effect,' wrote Vever. A skilful technician, Lalique used the same means of reduction as those employed in the creation of medals. This process, starting from a wax or plaster model of much larger proportions, enabled him to obtain an extreme delicacy of execution, down to the finest details. But Lalique's outstanding success, not only in Paris but in Turin (1902), Saint Louis (1904) and Liège (1905) did not stop him from gradually abandoning jewellery, until, from 1910, he devoted himself to glassware, beginning the second stage of his dazzling career. The fame of Lalique should not be allowed to eclipse that of his emulators. From 1889 the Vever brothers, Paul (1851-1915) and Henri (1854-1942) established themselves as the leading exponents of the new concepts, enlisting the assistance of Eugène Grasset, the author of several works on plants and their ornamental applications. Feminine myth also occupied an important place in their work, assuming a form that was poetic in its associations rather than dream-like or perverse. A pendant known as *Sylvia*, one of the masterpieces of Art Nouveau jewellery, bears witness to the perfection of an art based on elegance of design, refinement in the use of colour and the juxtapositioning of tones. The Vevers also, with Louis Cartier, set the

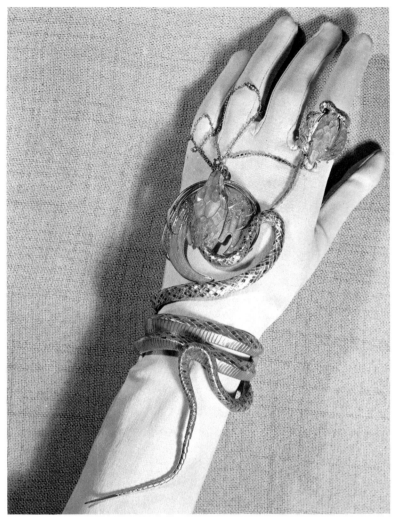

326 GEORGES FOUQUET Bracelet designed for Sarah Bernhardt by Alphonse Mucha. (Private Collection)

fashion for light, graceful settings of platinum, a metal previously reserved for fancy goods.

Georges Fouquet (1862-1957) created his own models, sometimes with the aid of other fashionable artists such as Desroziers, an ex-pupil of Grasset and in particular Alfonse Mucha (1860-1939), of Czech origin. Sarah Bernhardt, one of Mucha's greatest admirers, ordered from him not only posters, but extravagant jewellery to wear on the stage, such as the famous snake bracelet designed for the role of Cleopatra and ostentatious adornments linked with the form of her dress.

The rather more discreet jewellery of Lucien Gaillard (1861-n.d.) was inspired by Japanese art. In order to understand further the techniques, he brought a number of craftsmen to Paris, shortly after 1900, from Tokyo, who specialised in metals, enamels and lacquers. Eugène Feuillâtre (1870-1916) experimented with enamelled silver, using a difficult technique that permitted no more than a range of cold tones. André-Fernand Thesmar (1843-1912), specialised in sculpture and enamels, and in particular translucent cloisonné enamels, coloured with metallic oxides. Lucien Gautrait specialised in metal crafts and executed for Gariod a number of models that took up fashionable themes.

Most of the Art Nouveau artists designed not only jewellery but also combs, walking-stick knobs, tie pins, lorgnettes, fans,

327

328

327 **RENE LALIQUE** Blue enamelled gold brooch with ivory figures attributed to Rodin.
328 **RENE LALIQUE** Gold, silver and enamel brooch.

watches and cigarette boxes. Amongst many others, one can cite the names of Plumet, Prouvé, Guimard, Carabin, Colonna, Dabault, Tonnellier and Selmersheim. 'Immediately after the 1900 Exhibition,' wrote Emile Sedeyn, 'everybody set about designing jewellery: painters, sculptors and active young ladies who, the year before, had discovered poker-work or repoussé leather.'

This widespread, exultant creativity could not detract from the brilliant and often very different talents that began to emerge across Europe. The Belgian, Philippe Wolfers (1858-1929), borrowed his themes from nature, transposing flowers, dragonflies and butterflies into mildly stylised arabesques. Like Lalique, Wolfers knew how to manipulate his materials, creating reflections and transparent effects and bringing a wide range of colours into play. In 1893, at Anvers, Wolfers presented a number of works sculpted in ivory from the Congo, that had been offered to a number of artists by Leopold II. The rare jewels created by Henry van de Velde, the celebrated architect and decorator, reflect his liking for simplified, geometric structures.

England and Scotland rejected the lyricism of French jewellery in favour of the fragile, elegant creations of the Macdonald sisters of the Glasgow group and the severely ornamental style of Alexander Fisher and Charles Robert Ashbee. In Germany and Austria another kind of abstraction was evolving which prefigured the Cubists and the Decorative Arts style of the 20s. This aesthetic was being developed in Vienna, Darmstadt and in particular at Pforzheim, the centre of Jugendstil jewellery. Cranach, Otto Czeschka, Muller, Ferdinand Hauser, Josef Hoffmann and Koloman Moser were primarily architects and decorators, having for the most part participated in the Secessionist movement, founded in Vienna in 1897. They applied to jewellery the same theories that had served for furniture, architecture and various objects. Naturalistic themes were rare and always heavily stylised. This taste for balanced geometric constructions was opposed to the arabesques and abundant imagination of the French. Scandinavia was not untouched by this renewal. The jewellery of Georg Jensen (1866-1935), in silver incrusted with amber, opal and semi-precious stones was much in advance of its time. It also, however, contained 'barbarous' elements and much of its charm lies in this ambiguity. In the United States, Louis Comfort Tiffany revived traditional methods with his jewellery made by hand and embellished with cabochon stones.

In France, popular jewellery alone remained Art Nouveau in style until 1914 and even later since by 1905 it had been abandoned by the jewellery makers of repute. Colette, evoking Jean Lorrain, who had launched Lalique, expressed horror at his taste for 'cheap regalia, turbid gems of chalcedony, chrysoprase, opal and olivine, and fat rings of tortured gold, not fit to be seen, yet displayed with relish'.

329

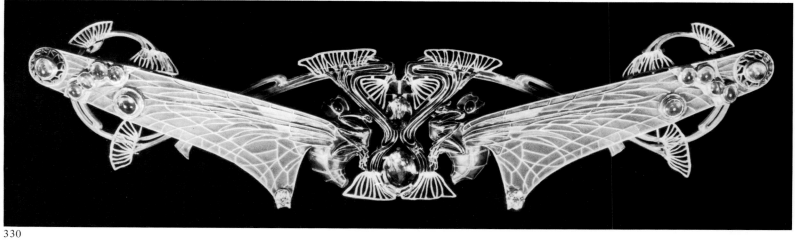

330

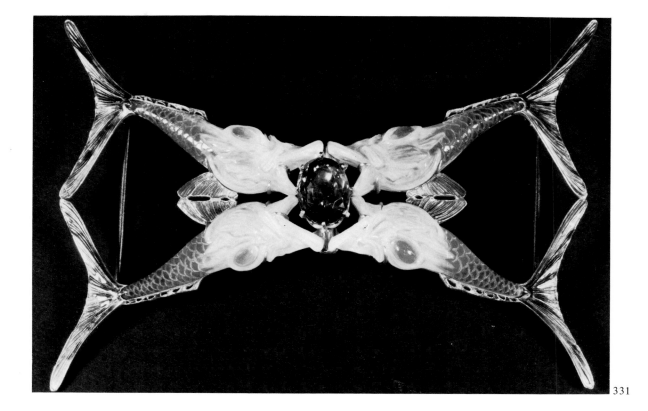

331

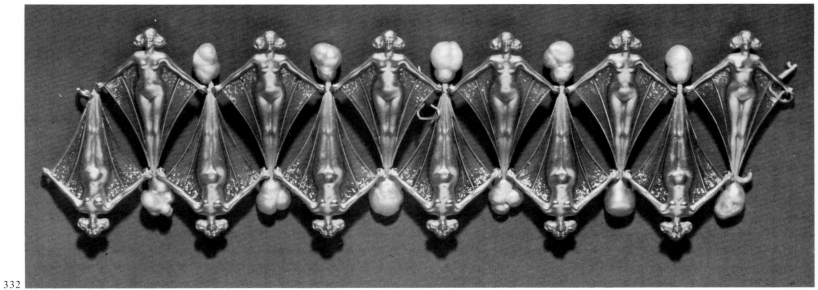

332

333

334

329 RENE LALIQUE Engraved glass bird with flowers of opal and blue enamel inset with sapphires.

330 RENE LALIQUE Two red-brown translucent enamel butterflies. (Private Collection)

331 RENE LALIQUE Pâte-de-verre fish holding in the centre a sapphire. (Private Collection)

332 RENE LALIQUE Bracelet in gold and enamel with baroque pearls.

333 RENE LALIQUE Carved ivory and opal pendant representing a woman whose hair becomes a mass of flowers, whose arms become birds and whose legs become wings. (Private Collection)

334 RENE LALIQUE Gold, translucent enamel and pâte-de-verre choker with cut and enamelled crystal and diamonds. (Private Collection.)

CASKETS

335 GABRIEL ARGY-ROUSSEAU Cigarette box in pâte-de-cristal. (Collection
Félix Marcilhac, Paris)

336 EMILE GALLE Workbox with fruitwood marquetry. (Musée de l'Ecole de
Nancy)

337 EMILE GALLE Glass casket.

336

337

LIGHTING

A new art of lighting was born with electricity, but this was hardly made apparent much before 1900. The incandescent lamp, which Edison was perfecting during the 1880s and displayed at the 1889 Exhibition, was above all a curiosity. Gas, paraffin oil, methylated spirit and even candles were still universally employed. Confronted by the problem of a new technique, the creators hesitated in the face of the difficulties of adaptations. Should one bring out the 'utilitarian machine' aspect, as had van de Velde at the request of Bing, or plump for a compromise in the composite Napoleon III style? After a number of abortive starts, electric lighting, in the form of lamps, chandeliers and bracket lamps finally got off the ground with the International Exhibition and the dazzling enchantment of its Palais de l'Electricité. Glass craftsmen, sculptors and decorators vied with each other to create the best inventions.

LAMPS

338

The brilliance of the light source intensified the glistening effects of coloured glass and the glass craftsmen exploited this delightful property to the full. Emile Gallé and the Daum brothers remained faithful, in this field, to naturalistic inspiration. Their love of flowers and plants was expressed in the form or in the ornamentation. In the former instance, the stylised line corresponds closely with the true appearance as in the corolla lamp, the three mushroom lamp, the palm-tree lamp etc. The movement of a petal suggests real life and the lighting brings out the delicacy of veins and nervures simulating in glass the tissue of the plant and accentuating its transparent qualities. Less elaborate lamps formed simply by a hood and vertical support, were equally inspired by floral and symbolist themes. The ornamentation covers the shade and sometimes the support, modelled in the same material to underline the unity of conception. Gallé also had a liking for twilight themes, thus transforming a utilitarian device into a decorative object.

The American, Tiffany was one of the first creators of incandescent lamps in the United States. Skilled in both metal and glass, he combined glass with bronze for his mosaic lampshades, mounting fragments of vividly coloured glass in a tracery of bronze thread, in the manner of cloisonné enamels. These lamps, distributed in Paris by Bing were immensely successful.

A number of lamp-statuettes, rich in invention, were executed in metal by sculptors. The *Loie Fuller* by Raoul Larche, brought back to life, in a swirl of draperies, the style of a dancer and the charm of an epoch. Emmanuel Frémiet (1824-1910) produced some zoomorphic lamps in which detailed observation and humour both hold sway. Georges de Feure, working in bronze, formed arabesques based on the stems of plants, with stylised deliberation.

338 CHERET Silvered metal and alabaster lamp. (Collection Félix Marcilhac, Paris)

339 EMILE GALLE Lamp in the shape of a mushroom with a base of wrought-iron. (Collection Félix Marcilhac, Paris)

340 EMILE GALLE Desk lamp in the form of an iris. (Musée des Arts Décoratifs, Paris)

341 EMILE GALLE Silvered metal lamp stand with glass shade.

339

340

341

342

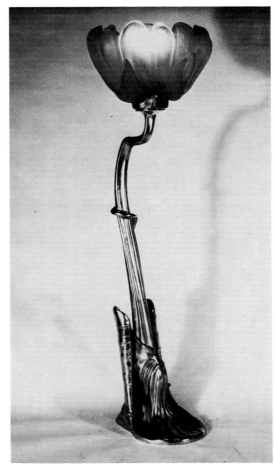

343

344

342 DAUM   Tall lamp. (Private Collection)

343 DAUM and LOUIS MAJORELLE   Waterlily lamp.

344 DAUM   Mushroom shaped lamp. (Collection Félix Marcilhac, Paris)

345

347

346

345-346 DAUM and LOUIS MAJORELLE Lamps which are closer in date to 1925 than 1900. (Private Colletion)

347 DAUM Night light in the shape of a poppy with insects attached to the flower. (Private Collection)

348

349

350

351

348 MAURICE BOUVAL Lamp in the form of cow-parsley. (Private Collection)

349 LOUIS MAJORELLE Wrought-iron lamp. (Musée de l'Ecole de Nancy)

350 TIFFANY Patinated bronze and iridescent glass lamp. (Collection Félix Marcilhac, Paris)

351 BRANDT and LANDRY Lamp. (Collection Knut Günther)

352 EMILE GALE Gilt-bronze lamp.

353 SARREGUEMINES Ceramic lamp, the light bulb being concealed in the drapery above the woman's head.

354 EMMANUEL VILLANIS Large bronze lamp stand.

355 CHAPELLE and MULLER Wrought-iron and coloured glass lamp. (Collection Alain Lesieutre, Paris)

352

353

354

355

BRACKET LAMPS

A highly baroque sense of fantasy was applied to this type of lighting. Sculptors, in particular, devoted themselves to the exploration of variations on floral themes. Jean Dampt respected the natural appearance of the flower and did not attempt to conceal the light bulb, which was treated as an integral part of the decoration. A similar approach was adopted by de Feure, Colonna, Selmersheim and many others. A picturesque, anecdotal style survived in some models: naiads surrounded by reeds and chubby infants blowing into corollas formed links between the charm of the Ancien Régime and the aesthetic of Art Nouveau.

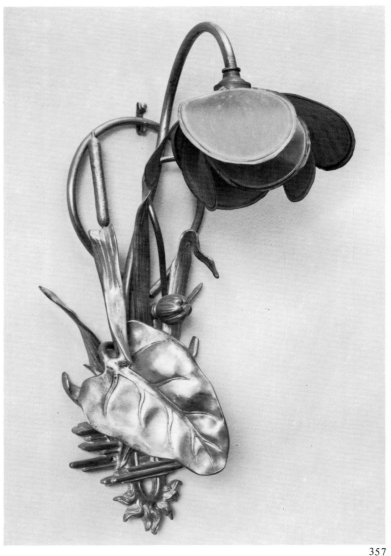

357

356

358

356 EMILE GALLE Wall bracket lamp. (Collection M. and Mme B.)

357 Gilt-bronze bracket lamp in the shape of a water-plant. (Private Collection)

358 EMILE ROBERT Wrought-iron bracket lamp (Musée des Arts Décoratifs, Paris)

359

360

361

362

359 JOSEPH CHERET Bracket lamp. (Collection Alain Lesieutre, Paris)

360 Bracket lamp of a nymph entitled *Naïade surgissant des eaux parmi les roseaux et les nénuphars.*

361-362 Gilt-bronze bracket lamps.

363 Bracket lamp entitled *Belle Epoque*. (Collection M. Abdy)

364-365 JOSEPH CHERET Bracket lamps in gilt-bronze and blue enamel. (Musée des Arts Décoratifs, Paris)

363

364

365

HANGING LAMPS

The designers applied their inventive skills to chandeliers and hanging lamps, an integral part of Art Nouveau decoration, with equal verve. Crystal still had its adepts, as was demonstrated, in 1900, by the exhibition of a magnificent chandelier by Baccarat and the creations of Lalique. Audacious innovators, such as Jean Dampt and Serrurier, treated the chandelier as a bouquet of luminous bronze flowers, in which the light bulb is displayed as an essential part of the decoration. In the dining room, the chandelier was often replaced by a hanging lamp. Sumptuous tulips, their cups inverted, drew on all the resources of coloured glass and the ornamental repertoire of the times. Their tinted light must have represented a rejection of the disagreeably dazzling effects of the incandescent lamp, an approach which strikes us today as surprising.

366 DAUM and MAJORELLE Hanging lamp. (Collection Félix Marcilhac, Paris)

367 JEAN DAMPT Light in the form of flowers.

366

367

368

369

368 EUGENE VALLIN Light from the dining room in Nancy. (Musée de l'Ecole de Nancy)

369 Ceiling lamp concealed behind crystal rods and balls. (Collection Alain Lesieutre, Paris)

370 *Boule de gui*, hanging lamp.

371 Lamp with dragonflies. (Collection Manoukian, Paris)

370

371

STANDARD LAMPS

The standard lamp, a traditional element in drawing-room furniture, kept pace with changing fashion. Artistic imagination was sometimes concentrated on the support and some-times on the shade, which Tiffany, in particular, created in terms of a mosaic of coloured glass.

372 Copper standard lamp once in the possession of Sarah Bernhardt. (Private Collection)
373 Wrought-iron standard lamp made in Japan for the European market. (Private Collection)

372

373

374

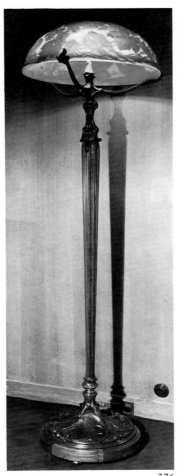

375

376

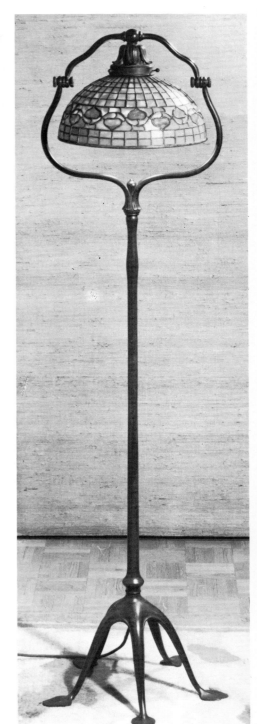

377

378

374 HECTOR GUIMARD Standard lamp. (Collection Manoukian, Paris)

375 LOUIS COMFORT TIFFANY Lamp. (Galerie du Luxembourg, Paris)

376 Tall standard lamp

377 LOUIS COMFORT TIFFANY Wrought-iron standard lamp. (Collection Alain Lesieutre, Paris)

378 DAUM Standard lamp with pink shade and green base. (Collection Jean-Claude Brugnot)

WROUGHT-IRON

The decorative possibilities of metal in an architectural context, which had been realised for the first time by Horta, in Brussels, were also explored enthusiastically by French craftsmen. We have already seen how wrought-iron was combined with glass to effect a renewal of the art of lighting. But its real vocation lay in items of ironwork conceived on a grand scale — entrance gates, banisters, balconies — and it was in this domaine that the potential of wrought-iron was most fully realised. The ironworker, like the cabinet-maker, ceramist and glass craftsman, was inspired by nature and replaced classical motifs with metallic flowers, springing up from stems twisted into volutes. In this way a style was created that has won its place in the history of art.

379 EMILE GALLE Wrought-iron lighting.

380 LOUIS MAJORELLE Fire dogs. (Musée de l'Ecole de Nancy)

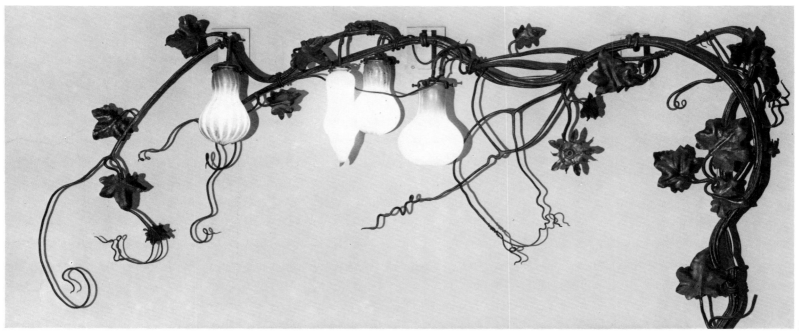

379

380

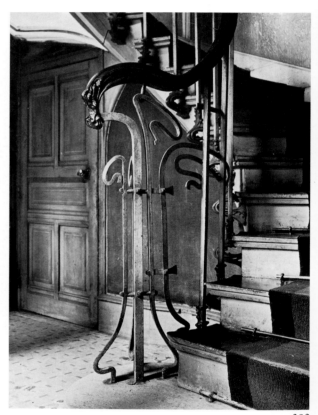

381

384

383

381 LOUIS MAJORELLE Banister. (Musée des Arts Décoratifs, Paris)

382 Balcony. (Musée de l'Ecole de Nancy)

383 Wrought-iron banister in a house on the rue Fontaine, Paris.

384 Balcony, rue Périchon.

ARCHITECTURE

With the Métro gratings of Hector Guimard, Art Nouveau had descended into the streets. It was only to be expected that it should rise up to claim the façades of the buildings and this it did, breaking all the rules and shattering the classical line to impose its curves and volutes in a plethora of sculptures. Stone ceased to be simply a material of construction and gave birth, beneath the artist's chisel to flowers, symbolic animals and the bodies of women. And to complete these schemes the architects, not content at having redesigned the entrance gates and balconies, went so far as to add climbing plants in cast-iron covering the full height of the façade.

385 Stone and bronze façade of a building on the avenue Wagram, Paris.

386 Detail of the same building.

385

386

387

388

389

390

387 HECTOR GUIMARD Entrance gate, rue La Fontaine.

388 Detail of a magnificent façade overflowing with bronze animals and foliage, rue d'Abbeville.

389 Door ornamented with ears of corn on the rue de Jeu-de-l'Arc, Geneva.

390 JULES LAVIROTTE Front porch on the avenue Rapp, dated 1898.

391

392

393

391 Detail of a large statue, rue d'Abbeville.

392-394 Façade and details of a building on the rue de Jeu-de-l'Arc, Geneva, ornamented with bunches of flowers, allegories and foliated scrolls carved from stone.

394

INDEX